Agatha Christie

Agatha Christie

First Lady of Crime

Edited by
H.R.F. KEATING

Holt, Rinehart and Winston
New York

823.09
A

Library of Congress Cataloging in Publication Data:

Agatha Christie: first lady of crime.

   I.   Christie, Agatha Miller, Dame, 1891-1976—
Addresses, essays, lectures.   2.   Authors, English—
20th century—Biography—Addresses, essays, lectures.
I.   Keating, Henry Reymond Fitzwalter, 1926-
PR6005.H66Z554   823'.9'12   76-29907
ISBN 0-03-018251-4

Designers: Tim Higgins and Sandra Shafee
Printed in Great Britain
10 9 8 7 6 5 4 3 2 1

Contents

Acknowledgments

Photographs and illustrations are supplied by or reproduced by kind permission of the following:
BBC Copyright Photograph: 71 (right); BFI Stills Library: 165, 166; British Library: 98 (above & below left); British Lion: 47, 199; Camera Press: 30 (photo: Bassano), 77 (photo: Snowdon); Collins (William), Sons & Co., Ltd: 16, 20, 62-3 (above), 98 (right); EMI Film Distributors Ltd: 17, 168, 179, 180, 181, 213 (below); Hamburger TV: 157; Keystone: 104-5, 109, 153; Mander and Mitchenson Theatre Collection: frontispiece, 14, 46, 53, 56, 57, 64, 70, 136, 137, 144, 145, 146-7, 149 (above), 212, 213 (above); MGM: 176;
National Film Archive: 158, 159, 160, 163; Popperfoto: 22-3, 67, 72, 73, 74, 75, 149 (below), 152, 186; Radio Times Hulton Picture Library: 58, 59, 62 (left), 63 (below), 71 (left); Sunday Telegraph: endpapers (cartoon by Nicolas Bentley); United Artists Corporation Ltd: 170, 171; Warner-Pathé: 167.
Jacket photography: Popperfoto

Picture research: Philippa Lewis
Film stills supplied by Philip Jenkinson

All possible care has been taken in making acknowledgment for the use of copyright material in this book. If any owner has not been acknowledged the publishers apologize and will be glad of the opportunity to rectify the error.

Introduction

AGATHA CHRISTIE was a phenomenon. She took a fairly simple form of entertainment, moderately popular at the time, and through it she made herself into a name known from China (where they preached at her rather puritanically) to Nicaragua (where they put Poirot on a postage stamp), selling in the course of it all more books than anyone has been able to count, getting translated into no fewer than 103 foreign languages (fourteen more than Shakespeare), writing a play that has run on the London stage longer than any other work of dramatic fiction ever, becoming (to speak crudely for a moment) the richest writer Britain has ever had, going confidently on from one generation to the next (I myself learnt of her at my mother's waist, if not knee; my children in turn have fallen victim to her wiles, as deceived as ever I was) and finally bringing to her art the same respectability that a knighted Irving brought to those actor rogues when, in 1971, she was made a Dame of the British Empire. She was beyond doubt the First Lady of Crime.

How did she do it? She lived an ordinary enough life; she was not in herself a particularly extraordinary person, though she was a more private one than most if hardly 'a figure of mystery'. Yet she achieved truly extraordinary feats. A mystery! And the answer to that mystery lies, beyond doubt, in another mystery. A mystery in the ancient sense of 'a handicraft or trade'. For, though her enormous success derived in part from our twentieth-century craving for easy images to grasp, so that 'Agatha Christie' became world-wide mental shorthand for 'mystery books', her writing itself certainly has exceptional virtues. A vessel that can take hurricane winds in her sails must be a sturdy barque indeed.

Her books, in common with almost all others of the kind, appeal of course to certain fundamentals shared by us all from Greenland's icy mountains to India's coral strand. They tickle that 'passion for hunting something deeply implanted in the human breast' which Dickens wrote of; their very nature proclaims, albeit entertainingly, that justice will prevail and evil can be conquered even by one man's effort; in a world increasingly swept by the irrational they quietly defend rationality; they appeal with their inevitable answer to the question 'Who done it?' to our deep-buried feeling for form. Indeed, perhaps no other writer in the genre has given us so many times that click of satisfaction when many seemingly loose ends fall at last neatly into place as Agatha Christie. Not unknowingly did she contrive even that her eightieth title came to us on her eightieth birthday.

But such factors account only for the firm basis of her extraordinary success. Her particular triumph comes, I believe, from the very ordinariness that would seem to preclude it. A middle-of-the-road person herself, she wrote about people who possessed those qualities we almost all share. Even Poirot, with a good claim to be among the most eccentric of fictional detectives, is in fact a well-judged *omnium gatherum* of what the ordinary person might expect an eccentric to be. It is not without significance that many of her characters over the years were brought to life by comparing them to man's friend, the dog – the lugubrious bloodhound, the persistent terrier.

Mrs Christie's virtue was that she stuck to her last. She did not go beyond those aspects of human nature that are our common stock. Very seldom, if ever, did she deviate even by a hair's breadth from the strict bounds that her story set for her, and that made her a splendidly direct and effective story-teller. She never succumbed to the temptation that lurks for every author in the popular vein, writers who in the nature of things are generally more gifted than the bulk of their readers, the temptation to shoot off one or two intellectual rockets, or a whole fusillade. She never tried to be clever in her writing, only ingenious in her plots. She knew, too, from the sympathy she had for ordinary people, at just what moment they needed each piece of information to build up the story she was telling. She served her public.

I see her in her writings as a circus clown, an entertainer linked magically to the surrounding spectators, and producing for them gifts essentially simple but none the less welcome for that. And welcome to all of us, save the most critical in their spikily critical hours. Out of the battered bowler hat or the conical cap comes the expected, long waited-for silk handkerchief – at exactly the right moment, in neatly the unexpected colour. We clap. We can't help it.

Yet her mystery deserves a more prolonged consideration than this. Thoroughly to explain it we need a diversity of approaches. And that is what is presented here. It is fashionable in French intellectual circles currently – and there can be no more intellectual circles than those, nor any more fashion-conscious – to claim that the many-angled approach of many writers is the highest form of biography, the *colloque*. I hardly go as far as that in putting forward this combined look at the phenomenon of Agatha Christie, that least intellectual of persons. But it is perhaps true that her mystery is best solved not, alas, by the lone amateur detective but by the sober and concerted efforts of all the specialists a whole police force can bring to bear. Let us see then what solution they produce.

H.R.F. KEATING

Elizabeth Walter

The Case of the Escalating Sales

ON 27 MAY 1926, two weeks after the end of the General Strike, when England was thankfully returning to normal and one or two of the forethoughtful were wondering if it would be worth saving for posterity copies of Churchill's emergency *British Gazette*, an event of more enduring literary significance occurred: *The Murder of Roger Ackroyd* was published.

It was not Agatha Christie's first novel, but it was the one which made her name, for the audacious ingenuity of its ending had critics and public divided on the issue of 'Was it fair?' It was also the first of her books to be published by Collins, and marked the beginning of an author–publisher relationship which endured for fifty years and well over seventy books.

When in the 1920s Sir Godfrey Collins and his editorial director, Mr F. T. Smith, began to build up a trade list in London for what had hitherto been a Glasgow-based publishing house chiefly distinguished for Bibles, educational books and the Collins Classics, they included among their early acquisitions a number of detective novels by authors such as Freeman Wills Crofts, G. D. H. Cole, Philip Macdonald, and others less well remembered. They sold satisfactorily. The up-and-coming publishers were therefore delighted when the literary agents Hughes Massie approached them with a script by Agatha Christie, an up-and-coming author who was already published by John Lane (Bodley Head). The script was so good that Collins eagerly entered into a three-book contract dated 27 January 1924, even though there were two books still to come from the Bodley Head. Two years later, *The Murder of Roger Ackroyd* was published at 7s 6d.

The thirty-four-year-old Mrs Christie was not an unknown quantity. Her first book, *The Mysterious Affair at Styles*, featuring a little Belgian detective named Hercule Poirot, had sold a mere 2,000 copies, but she was also well known as a writer of detective short stories. In 1923, when the weekly *Sketch* published a series of them, a whole page of pictures was devoted to the author at home, at her typewriter, on the telephone, or with her small daughter. Hughes Massie, her agents then as now, thought that Collins with their accent on detective fiction would be the ideal publisher in Britain. They were proved right. *The Murder of Roger Ackroyd* was published in a first edition of approximately 5,500 copies*, and rapidly sold over 4,000 of these – considered then a very good sale. In America Agatha Christie was published from the first by Dodd, Mead.

* Approximate because Collins's detailed sales records were unfortunately destroyed during the Blitz.

The Maker of "The Grey Cells of M. Poirot."

At the telephone.

With her daughter, Rosalind: Agatha Christie, the great detective-story writer.

At her writing table.   At work with her type-writer.

In her drawing-room: the author of the series of detective stories we begin this week.

With "Tutankhamen cushions: Agatha Christie and her little girl.

CREATOR OF THE MOST INTERESTING DETECTIVE SINCE SHERLOCK HOLMES: AGATHA CHRISTIE.

Agatha Christie (who is in private life Mrs. Archibald Christie, the mother of a charming little daughter, Rosalind) is the brilliant writer of detective fiction, and creator of Hercule Poirot, the most fascinating character any novel-reader could wish to meet. Her first book, "The Mysterious Affair at Styles," introduced Poirot, the detective who, by the aid of what he calls "those brave little grey cells" of his brain, unravels the strangest tangles of crime. A series of stories dealing with Poirot's further exploits has been written for "The Sketch," and opens this week—on the page opposite. The tales are a thrilling set of detective yarns which equal anything ever published in that style.

PHOTOGRAPH BY ALFIERI SPECIALLY TAKEN FOR "THE SKETCH."

Perhaps emboldened by this, Collins were able to make the following claim for their crime fiction in their catalogue for autumn 1926: 'We realize that the success of a Detective Novel depends upon the ingenuity and infallible accuracy of the author in the handling of his plot. We realize, too, that mere sensation based on irrelevant episodes will never make a good detective novel. We have accordingly set a very high standard. Only the best will do. That is why we have today the finest list of Detective Novels in existence.'

Despite the furore caused by *The Murder of Roger Ackroyd*, there was no reprint during the first year of publication, and the days when first printings would be ten times that initial figure were still far ahead. But a few months after publication an event occurred which was to have a profound – though not entirely favourable – effect on Agatha Christie's future career. She disappeared.

Suddenly the missing mystery writer was headline news, her name known throughout the country. Inevitably, there were those who said – unfairly – that it was a publicity stunt. Equally unfairly, there is no denying that the disappearance did indeed have a considerable effect on the sales of her next books. *The Big Four* (1927), which is really a collection of four linked short stories, sold over 8,500. *The Mystery of the Blue Train* (1928), based on a short story entitled 'The Mystery of the Plymouth Express' and described by Agatha Christie herself as 'easily the worst book I ever wrote', dropped to just below 7,000. *The Seven Dials Mystery* (1929), a sequel to an earlier book, *The Secret of Chimneys*, neither of them typical Christie, rose again to over 8,000. There can be few better examples of the effect of press publicity. Its ethics are another matter.

The year 1930 was a momentous one both for Agatha Christie personally and for the house of Collins. In September Mrs Christie, by now divorced, married the archaeologist Max Mallowan and began a life of great personal happiness. As if in celebration, the same year saw the publication of *Murder at the Vicarage*, the first book under a new six-book contract with Collins, in which Miss Jane Marple was introduced. For Collins, 1930 saw the birth of the Crime Club, the brainchild of Sir Godfrey and his nephew, young William Collins, who felt that the vogue for the detective story and the enormous popularity of book clubs could profitably be linked. Not that the Crime Club was ever a book club; simply the imprint under which Collins publish crime fiction. The first title was *The Noose*

In 1923, Agatha Christie was becoming well known as a writer of detective short stories, and *The Sketch*, in devoting a whole page of pictures to the author at home, referred to the 'thrilling set of detective yarns' that she had written.

Same time next year? A display window (*above*) at Collins the publishers,
proclaiming the effective slogan 'The latest Agatha Christie';
the 1974 *Murder on the Orient Express* was a film that was as lavish
a production as its star-studded poster (*right*) suggests, but the Christie
phenomenon never needed to rely on such publicity for its momentum.

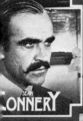

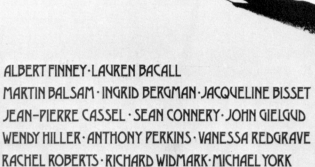

by Philip Macdonald, with a first printing of approximately 5,500. A few months later came *Murder at the Vicarage*. But by now the publicity bonanza was over and the first printing was back to 5,500. Agatha Christie did not shoot to best-sellerdom overnight.

It was not until *Three Act Tragedy* in 1935 (*Murder in Three Acts* in America) that she managed to sell 10,000 within the first year of publication, and 1943 before she reached 20,000 with *Five Little Pigs* (*Murder in Retrospect* in America) – perhaps a result of wartime dependence on the printed word for entertainment. Thereafter she never looked back and the Agatha Christie phenomenon becomes the Case of the Escalating Sales, with *Sparkling Cyanide*, called in America *Remembered Death* (1945), selling 30,000 within twelve months, and *The Hollow*, America's *Murder After Hours*, touching 40,000 in the following year. By 1950, when her fiftieth book, *A Murder Is Announced*, was published, the first printing was 50,000 and her subsequent crime books have never sunk below that figure. *Passenger to Frankfurt*, the 'extravaganza', as she called it, published to coincide with her eightieth birthday, beat all records, for by the end of the first year there were 58,000 copies in print. *Sleeping Murder*, the last Christie thriller of all and the final Miss Marple story, had a first printing of 60,000.

Despite the publicity attached to the recent star-studded film *Murder on the Orient Express*, Agatha Christie's success was never dependent on such outside stimulants. It is doubtful if the early plays and films based on her books significantly affected her sales. Until the outbreak of war in 1939 only two of her books had been dramatized – *Alibi* in 1928, from *The Murder of Roger Ackroyd*, and *Love from a Stranger* in 1936, based on the short story 'Philomel Cottage'; this was also filmed in 1937. But if stage and screen had less effect in the thirties than they do today, the coming of paperbacks introduced Agatha Christie to a new, avid and very faithful audience.

When Allen Lane founded Penguin Books in 1935, he was able to renew an old acquaintance, for he had handled Agatha Christie's early hardback books while working for his uncle John Lane at the Bodley Head. Now two of these early Christie titles, *The Mysterious Affair at Styles* and *Murder on the Links*, were among the fifteen original titles in the famous greenback crime series, Agatha Christie and Dorothy L. Sayers being the only two authors to be represented by two books each. In a surprisingly short time, Agatha Christie had become the first author after Bernard Shaw and H. G. Wells to have a million paperback copies of her books published on one day. Since then she has been published in Britain by Fontana, Pan and Penguin, and her books are reprinted constantly. In America, too, she has had several paperback publishers, among them Dell and Pocket Books.

By 1955 she had become a limited company, Agatha Christie Ltd. In 1968 the company was acquired by Booker Books, a subsidiary of Booker Brothers McConnell, who were anxious to diversify their traditional shipping, sugar-growing and rum-distilling interests. They had already acquired Ian Fleming, author of the James Bond books. Now, once again, they took a 51 per cent stake in the future work of a best-selling author – and they chose well. Even so, Agatha Christie remarked in 1970 that if she wrote more than one book a year she would only enlarge the finances of the Inland Revenue, 'who would spend it mostly on idiotic things'.

In 1965, inspired by the author's seventy-fifth birthday, Collins decided to bring out a collected edition of her works. The name Greenway Edition was chosen for the series, after Greenway House, Agatha Christie's Devonshire home. The first four titles were *The Labours of Hercules*, *Crooked House* (Agatha Christie's own favourite among her books), *A Murder Is Announced*, and of course *The Murder of Roger Ackroyd*.

Collins also published or republished a number of titles which do not fall within the Christie crime canon. These include *Star over Bethlehem* (1965), a collection of stories and poems for children, all with religious themes; a volume of autobiography, *Come, Tell Me How You Live*, originally published in 1946 and reprinted in 1975; six romantic novels under the name Mary Westmacott, originally published between 1930 and 1956 and republished in a uniform edition in 1973 and 1974; a play, *Akhnaton* (1973); and *Collected Poems* (1973), which contained her earlier volume of verse, *The Road of Dreams*, originally published in 1925 by Geoffrey Bles.

To a publisher's eye, she was one of the most professional of authors. Her typescripts arrived when she said they would. Her proofs were promptly corrected and returned. She did not care for any editing of her text, and as late as 1968 she wrote to Sir William Collins asking him to ensure that the spelling she used would not be changed unless a word had actually been misspelt; if there were two alternative spellings, she wanted her choice of spelling to be left alone. Similarly she objected to sentences being re-arranged to be more grammatically correct, especially in the case of spoken conversation, for this would make all the characters sound alike and not like ordinary variable human beings.

She liked to have a say in everything connected with her books, notably the jacket and the blurb. On one occasion, when by accident a jacket was not shown her, she wrote angrily protesting about this and saying that she wanted to see every jacket design before it was finalized because she hated having things put over on her. As this implies, she had strong views about jackets. She would never consent to any representation of Poirot, not even as played by Albert Finney in *Murder on the Orient Express*; and though she once allowed his patent-leather-shod feet to appear on the jacket of *Poirot's Early*

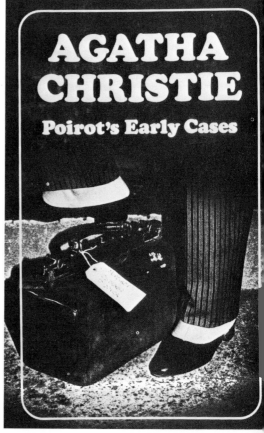

Left : One of the earliest (1924) jackets depicting Hercule Poirot; later his creator would not consent to any representation of the little Belgian detective, and she was even reluctant to allow his patent-leather-shod feet to appear on the jacket of *Poirot's Early Cases* (right).

Cases, she was never happy with even this partial representation. Her preference was always for a motif, and she herself drew the design for the three intertwined fish which appear on the jackets of the Greenway Edition.

She wrote fast and reckoned to complete a book in six weeks, working straight on to the typewriter and using three fingers instead of what she claimed was the more usual two, though her last few books were dictated straight on to the machine which Collins gave her for her eightieth birthday, because she had begun to find typing tiring. For a long time she averaged two books a year, and she maintained this output even during the war when circumstances such as paper shortage prevented such frequent publication. The result was two novels which she salted away, intending them to appear only after her death. In the case of *Curtain : Poirot's Last Case*, she was sufficiently impressed by the success of the film, *Murder on the Orient Express*, and the resulting interest in Poirot, to relent and allow it to be published in 1975.

Agatha Christie was a professional and she expected an equal degree of professionalism from her publishers. On one occasion – well remembered at Collins! – her author's copies of *Endless Night* failed to arrive before she left for a holiday in Spain. She wrote to say that she had been absolutely infuriated to see a whole array of *Endless Night* when she arrived at Heathrow airport and that, though she had found a parcel of books on her return home, these could hardly be called the author's 'advance copies'!

Besides a keen sense of what was properly due to an author, Agatha Christie was also very conscious of what was due to a work of creative imagination. She once replied to someone who wished to include an abridged passage from *The Body in the Library* in a modern language teaching series that, although it might be difficult for a person who was not himself an imaginative writer to appreciate, she felt making an abridged version of a creative author's book was like mutilating his brainchild. She said that she felt this to be true of any abridgement including recordings on tape. She did however allow her books to be serialized, and she was certainly aware of the difficulties of abridging, for she once tried to write a film version of her favourite Dickens novel, *Bleak House* – 'such a good plot' – and discovered ruefully: 'The amount of characters in that book! I found I had to cut out many of the best ones.'

Tea-table on the front lawn,
the idyllic setting of
Agatha Christie's Devonshire
home, Greenway House,
the name of which was chosen
for the collected edition
of her works that began
to be brought out in 1965,
the Greenway Edition.

Although she was one of the world's biggest sellers, outsold only by the Bible and Shakespeare, Agatha Christie was remarkably modest. She never expected the day's work at Collins to be abandoned because she had crossed the threshold, and far from her craving publicity, her experience of it after the alleged 'disappearance' of 1926 caused her to shun it. She would never make a speech in public, not even at the party Collins gave to celebrate her eightieth birthday, when the leading literary editors came to do her homage.

But despite her reticence, she had the essential self-possession that comes from being born into a comfortable level of society – perhaps one might best describe it as the 'officer class', for her brother went into the army after leaving Harrow, and her first husband was a colonel in the Royal Flying Corps. It was evidently a station of life which suited her: an appropriate setting for the bridge and crossword puzzles and gardening which she so enjoyed. Her letters to her

publishers give an occasional tantalizing glimpse of a comfortable way of life which, for all her vast earnings, never inclined to the ostentatious.

Nevertheless, within the limits of her secure and ordered world, Agatha Christie was always conscious of social change. 'When I re-read those first books,' she said in 1966, 'I'm amazed at the number of *servants* drifting about. And nobody is really doing any work, they're always having tea on the lawn.' In her fiftieth novel, *A Murder Is Announced*, she endeavoured to show some of the changes wrought in Miss Marple's village of St Mary Mead in the immediate post-war years. And the last book she wrote, *Postern of Fate*, published in 1974, contains a comment on one aspect of English life today which must have struck a responsive chord in many readers. 'He was used, now, to the general pattern of labour in the building trade, electrical trade, gas employees and others. They came, they showed efficiency, they made optimistic remarks, they went away to fetch something. They didn't come back. One rang up numbers on the telephone but they always seemed to be the wrong numbers. If they were the right numbers the right man was not working at this particular branch of the trade, whatever it was.'

Nor was her awareness of the need to move with the times confined to her books. In 1970 she wrote to her publisher saying that she had read a review of the Fontana series on Modern Masters. She asked if it would be possible to send her this series because she wanted to keep up to date and felt it would help her writing, and because she felt that Alexander *must* have an intelligent great-grandmother. The series includes such writers as Freud, Fanon, Chomsky and Wittgenstein. Alexander's great-grandmother was then eighty.

On 13 May 1976, exactly two weeks before the fiftieth anniversary of the first publication of *The Murder of Roger Ackroyd*, a memorial service for Agatha Christie was held at St Martin-in-the-Fields. At the request of her family, the address was given by Sir William Collins, her friend and publisher. It was the crowning tribute, on both sides, to a professional and personal relationship which had endured for half a century.

Julian Symons
The Mistress of Complication

I

FOR SOME YEARS the Detection Club of London held its occasional informal dinners – as distinct from the formal one at which new members were inducted each year by making responses to the club's ritual while they placed one hand upon a lighted skull – at a Soho restaurant. At one of these dinners I arrived late, and went straight into the dining-room, just in time to see the end of the soup. My seat was opposite that of the president, Agatha Christie, and as we ate the next course I became aware that her mild unemphatic gaze was often directed at . . . could it be my expanding but hardly visible waistline? Was there a mark on my tie? It took me a minute or two to realize that she was looking, in a speculative rather than a censorious way, at my hands, and that they were rather grubby.

As soon as I could easily do so I got up, washed my hands, and returned. There is no 'story' here, no comment was made, and I can offer nothing more than a personal conviction that Agatha Christie was viewing those grubby hands as a possible constituent element in some plot. *A man comes to table – his hands are grubby – faintly marked with some kind of stain – yet half a dozen people are prepared to say that he spent the whole day in his office . . .* I feel sure that some such thoughts were passing through her mind.

She said once that she thought of turns in her plots most often while eating apples in the bath, but what they evidently spring from is unusually keen observation. In many ways she was what she appeared to be, a middle-class English lady with highly conventional opinions, but she was something else too. The middle-class lady had a considerable knowledge of the ways in which poisons work, derived from her World War I experience as a nurse, and also a keen professional interest in motives for and methods of murder. In its concern with detail this interest rarely transgressed beyond the bounds of a middle-class lady's taste, and she would have felt it both unnecessary and unpleasant to describe the physical details of a violent crime, or the mental agony suffered by a victim of rape. Nobody is ever raped in an Agatha Christie story. Her attitude would have been that one knows such things happen, but that they were hardly suitable subjects for detective fiction. It was the plotting of crime that fascinated her, not its often unpleasant end, and it is as a constructor of plots that she stands supreme among modern crime writers. Raymond Chandler once said that plotting was a bore, a necessary piece of journeywork that had to be done, and that the actual writing was the thing that gave the author pleasure. Agatha Christie's feelings were almost the opposite of these, which is one reason why she didn't care for Chandler's work.

Her most stunningly original plots are those in *The Murder of Roger Ackroyd*, *The A.B.C. Murders* and *Ten Little Niggers* (also evasively called *And Then There Were None* and *Ten Little Indians*), but although these are her major achievements, she showed from the beginning an extraordinary assurance in handling the devices in a detective story plot.

Her first book, *The Mysterious Affair at Styles*, was published in 1920 but written some years earlier, when she was working in a Red Cross dispensary during World War I. It was written in response to a challenge by her sister, and Hercule Poirot was conceived in a determination to create a detective outside the Sherlock Holmes pattern. Physically outside the pattern at least, for Poirot has both his forerunner's mental acuity and his maddening zest for mystification. In general it is true that nothing becomes out-of-date more quickly than an old detective story but *Styles*, which was turned down by several publishers, remains wonderfully readable today. In part this is because of Poirot, but it is chiefly a tribute to the plot.

Most Christie plots are based upon a single and fairly simple circumstance, which is then elaborated and concealed. In *Styles* the plot springs from the fact that in England somebody acquitted of a crime may not be tried for it again. Suppose, then, that a stumbling block against your committing a murder is the fact that you are an obvious suspect, you might – if you have that particular kind of tortuously ingenious mind – take advantage of this very situation by laying a trail of clues leading to yourself, which would cause your arrest. Once arrested and tried you produce an alibi, and acquittal follows. This murder plan may seem unlikely, but it was carried through successfully in real life a decade after the publication of *Styles* by a murderer who confessed when there was little evidence against him, withdrew his confession at his trial, was acquitted for lack of other evidence, and then boasted of his crime. The Christie villain is foiled by Poirot, who sees what he is trying to do, manages to prevent his arrest, and even uncovers his alibi so that he is apparently cleared of suspicion. Poirot's manoeuvring also deceives the reader, who sees the detective proving a suspect's innocence, and so crosses him off the list of those who may have committed the crime.

There are other felicities in *Styles*, in particular several of those deductions that trick us by their very simplicity. The two significant facts, Poirot tells his Watsonic collaborator Captain Hastings, are that the thermometer registered eighty degrees in the shade on the day of the murder, and that the chief suspect wears odd clothes, has a black beard and uses glasses. We may say with Hastings: 'Poirot, I cannot believe you are serious', but the points are clear enough. (1) The murdered woman ordered a fire to be lighted in her room on this hot summer day: hence, she meant to burn something. (2) The suspect has been identified by the local chemist as a man who bought poison, but his peculiarities of appearance make him very easy to impersonate.

Styles was a splendid beginning. Not all of the books that succeeded it were on the same level, and the semi-thrillers that used what has been called a 'master criminal' theme seem to me inferior in almost every way to the orthodox detective stories. But as Agatha Christie's skills developed, a pattern emerged which might be called the typical Christie plot form. It was used by other people too, but by none so well or so variously as in her books. The form consisted of gathering a number of people together in a particular place preliminary to one of them being murdered, and of showing the reasons for their presence. It is a way of creating a totally closed society, and one can see it happening in very different books: *Death in the Clouds* (1935) (*Death in the Air* in America), *Cards on the Table* (1936), *Death on the Nile* (1937), and *Ten Little Niggers* (1939). To look at the way in which these plots are devised and carried through is to see the high skill that was, with almost deceptive casualness, employed in them.

Death in the Clouds gives us eleven passengers but only ten suspects, since the eleventh airplane passenger is Poirot. There they are, *en route* from Le Bourget to Croydon (in relation to air travel the book has a strong period flavour), and we get glimpses of their actions and thoughts. Among these glimpses are the thoughts, deceptively conveyed of course, of the murderer. The victim is Madame Giselle, she has a mark on her neck, and a wasp has been flying about in the cabin. Was the wasp responsible? But below one passenger's seat is a thorn of the kind used by South American tribes for puffing from

blowpipes. The thorn is tipped with curare, and a blowpipe is found under the seat of . . . Poirot.

There are two highly characteristic things about this outline of suspects and setting of a scene. The first is that it confines the suspects to the people on board the airplane and then, by a process of elimination, to those who got up and passed Madame Giselle's seat or had the chance to use a blowpipe; the second, that a trick is being used

A portrait taken in 1932, the year of publication of the sometimes underrated *Peril at End House*.

in the apparently simple outline. At an early point Poirot says that a detailed list of the passengers' belongings will help to solve the crime. We are given this list, which covers three pages, and yes, if we interpret it correctly we shall come up with the right answer. But the interpretation is not easy to make.

In *Cards on the Table* the situation is more deliberately artificial. The rich Mr Shaitana 'collects' undiscovered murderers on the ground that 'murder can be art! A murderer can be an artist'. These are, he says 'the ones who have got away with it, the criminals who lead an agreeable life which no breath of suspicion has ever touched'. Shaitana stages a dinner party to which he invites four detectives familiar to Christie readers – Superintendent Battle, Colonel Race, Mrs Ariadne Oliver and Poirot himself – and four murderers, or four people said by him to have committed murder. Some rubbers of bridge are played, and the evening ends with Shaitana's death. The closed circle is perfect. Veteran Christie readers know that the detectives are beyond suspicion. Which of the four bridge players is the killer? The bridge scores are reproduced at the beginning, and by studying them – and the text – it is possible to come up with the right answer.

Death on the Nile, Agatha Christie's own favourite among her books with a foreign setting, is a more subtle and sophisticated affair. In the first twenty-five pages we meet all the principal characters and discover their reasons, that is the reasons they give to each other, for going to Egypt. The murderer is among these characters, and again a careful reader of these opening pages may deduce correctly what is likely to follow. The deception here is one of the most brilliant pieces of Christie conjuring, because at a fairly early stage the intelligent reader may think he sees what is going to happen, only to be confounded when the crime is committed by the fact that what he suspected seems to be impossible. I should be inclined to put this with the very best Christie plots if she had not been so desperately intent to deceive as to strain credulity at times. Her party of travellers down the Nile includes a kleptomaniac, an alcoholic, a thief and a subsidiary would-be murderer whose activities have nothing to do with the main plot. All this is too much, and indeed is far more than was needed to achieve her ends. The true deceptions, those connected with the main plot, are puzzling enough, in particular one that concerns a pistol wrapped up in a cheap handkerchief and a velvet stole and thrown overboard. Why was this done, Poirot asks again and again, saying rightly that it is the crux of the case. In spite of the red herrings, for which she had perhaps rather too strong a liking, Agatha Christie's sense of fair play is always paramount in relation to a significant clue. She shows it to us, teases us with it, almost openly tells us the truth about it through Poirot – and still we are deceived because of her meticulous way with words, which when she is dealing with a clue in a story are to be taken precisely at their literal meaning. In *Death on the Nile* we see a pistol being fired, and we see the result as a crimson stain spreads over a wounded man's trouser leg, but . . . but close reading of the passage is advisable.

I shall have something to say about the plotting of *Ten Little Niggers* later on. Here it is enough to point out the skill with which, in the first section, the pattern is developed as the suspects who are also the victims are seen deciding to accept invitations to the island off the Devon coast where after dinner on the first evening all ten of them hear a recording which says that they were guilty of murder and asks: 'Prisoners at the bar, have you anything to say in your defence?' Again a trick, the first in a whole series, is being played on us. We are allowed to see some of the thoughts of the person who has devised this death trap without having much chance of placing a name to him or her. Except, of course, by a knowledge of Agatha Christie's methods, of the kind of trap she sets.

2

The kind of trap she sets – there are people who claim to be able always to tell the villain in any Christie story by such an awareness. I couldn't make this claim myself, and indeed I doubt whether it is possible to be specific about the 'kind of trap'. Even the pattern I have called the typical Christie plot form does not apply to the majority of her books, although it is used in a high percentage of the best ones. But her work is astonishingly varied. There is a whole slew of books that take their settings from the fact that her second husband Sir Max Mallowan is an archaeologist, concerned chiefly with Assyrian culture, and that she often accompanied him and to some extent shared his interests. But although archaeology has a place in several stories her readers are never oppressed by a feeling of ignorance. She had an instinctive awareness of just how far her audience would wish her to go in show-ing expert knowledge, and no Agatha Christie mystery depends for its solution on a knowledge of ancient artefacts. Even in *Death Comes as the End* (1945), a not very successful experiment set in ancient Egypt, no specialized knowledge is needed to solve the puzzle.

There are several other sets of books which don't fit into any particular pattern of plotting. These include the five Tommy and Tuppence thrillers, books such as *The Mysterious Mr Quin* in which Agatha Christie indulged her interest in the supernatural, and the collections of Poirot and Miss Marple short stories. All of these seem to me not only inferior to her best work, but also as remote from the main stream of it as are the romantic novels she wrote under the name of Mary Westmacott. The main stream of her writing is unquestionably in the thirty-odd Poirot novels and the much smaller number, eleven at my last count, concerned with Miss Marple.

One sees certain things more clearly in looking back at her work than was apparent when reading the books as they were published. One is the supremacy of the best Poirot stories over the rest of what she wrote. She became tired of Poirot herself and preferred Miss Marple, who did not appear in a novel until 1930, with the feeble *Murder at the Vicarage*. Miss Marple, she said, was more fun, and like many aunts and grandmothers was 'a splendid natural detective when it comes to observing human nature'. Only a minority of readers agreed with her. If one prefers Poirot it is not only because he is an altogether livelier character, but also because his insights are more rational and less inspirational than Miss Marple's. A second thing that becomes apparent is her frequent carelessness in leaving deplorably loose ends, and a third is the highly verbal nature of her plotting. It is not just that you don't need to know about ancient artefacts to solve a Christie puzzle, but that you need no specialized knowledge at all. Think of John Dickson Carr's locked room mysteries, of R. Austin Freeman's (and many another writer's) scientific lore, of the learning paraded by Dorothy L. Sayers, of all those crime stories that depend for their solution upon our technical knowledge of the theatre, or of bibliography, or on changes of temperature, or timetables, or tide tables, and the Christie simplicity will seem most welcome. Yet simplicity is not quite the word. The basic difference in plotting between her and most detective story writers is that the central clue in almost all of her best books is either verbal or visual. We are induced to give a meaning to something that has been said, or something that has been seen, which is not the true meaning or not the only possible meaning. A typical instance of the verbal illusion occurs in a story where we are led to believe that a child named Evelyn, born to a woman involved in a murder case, is a girl. But Evelyn may be a boy's name too. Why do we never think of that as a possibility? Because early in the story the mother gives a newspaper interview in the course of which she says: 'My daughter shall grow up happy and innocent. Her life shall not be tainted by the cruel past.' But we are told clearly enough in relation to the interview that the woman who gives it is *expecting* a child, so that she could not possibly have known its sex. The assumption has been planted in our minds, and when the woman's child Evelyn is mentioned, we take the feminine sex for granted. The assumption is unjustified. Evelyn is a man.

Visual deceptions are of the kind suggested already in relation to *Death on the Nile*. Sometimes it is hardly possible for us to penetrate them, but many have the marvellous conjurer's quality (*They Do It With Mirrors – Murder With Mirrors* in America – is of this kind) that leave one gasping with pleasure at the audacity of the deceiver, saying: 'So *that's* how it was done.' Such visual and verbal clues, when they are used with subtlety and fairness, seem to me the very best things in the classical detective story. At her best Dame Agatha Christie was an incomparable deceiver.

That the level of her work varied greatly has to be acknowledged. Most of her finest performances belong to the 1920s and 1930s. The following decade more or less maintained this high level, but after that the decline was steady and near the end it was steep. The books of her last few years were, with only one or two exceptions, no more than faint echoes of her best work. A book like *The Clocks* (1963) opens very promisingly with a body found in a room full of clocks, most of which have no right to be there. The explanation of this anomaly, which would have been the heart of an earlier novel, is both casual and disappointing. And the people have become shadowy too, as inevitably she lost touch with contemporary life and feeling.

A survey of her whole output shows that she was often slapdash from the beginning in dealing with the technical details from which she flinched. *Murder on the Links* (1923), for instance, has been justly praised for its complicated and brilliant plotting, and for the way in which details of a twenty-year-old murder are interwoven with a current one. It contains one of her most characteristically clever touches of deception, and what must be called an almost equally characteristic carelessness in handling an important plot detail. The touch of deception first. The question arises as to how some intruders left a house. Perhaps, Poirot suggests, they might have climbed on to a tree and jumped down to a flower-bed, but it is pointed out to him that the mould is perfectly smooth. A companion flower-bed, he says, shows marks of the gardener's hob-nailed boots, but the official investigator replies scornfully that on this side 'we have no tree, and consequently no means of gaining access to the upper storey'. When Poirot insists that the gardener's footprints are important he is thought ridiculous. What is their importance? Just that the gardener has weeded both beds, and so must have left his footprints on both. The fact that the second bed is smooth means that the intruders *did* escape that way, and that they had time to smooth the mould after them.

And now the piece of carelessness. At an early stage of the case Poirot picks up a piece of lead piping on the scene of a crime, and much later says that it has been used 'to disfigure the victim's face so that it would be unrecognizable'. But Hastings has already looked at the victim, and neither he nor the police investigator mentions the savage blows that would have been necessary to make the face unrecognizable. Hastings says that it was 'terribly convulsed', which is quite a different matter.

3

In the end Agatha Christie's claim to supremacy among the classical detective story writers of her time rests on her originality in constructing puzzles. This was her supreme skill, and it is examined here in three books, *The Murder of Roger Ackroyd*, *The A.B.C. Murders* and *Ten Little Niggers*. Some would add to these, which I regard as her most dazzling performances, *Murder on the Orient Express* (1934) (in the US *Murder in the Calais Coach*) or *Peril at End House* (1932) or even the last Poirot story *Curtain* (1975). But the crime writer who relies on a puzzle is like a tight-rope walker. A perfect achievement is a perfect marvel, but anything less, any slight swaying on the line, leaves us sharply critical. Both *Murder on the Orient Express* and *Curtain* are for me too obviously and purely tricks, and although I rate *Peril at End House* much more highly than do most critics, it cannot quite be ranked with Christie's best.

The Murder of Roger Ackroyd was published in 1926, and probably remains its author's most famous single work. She was inclined herself to say that too much fuss had been made about it, but that was at least in part the reaction of any writer who feels that praise of an early book implies denigration of later ones. But in *Roger Ackroyd* Agatha Christie did something absolutely new in the detective story. It was a plot device, and what can be *absolutely* new in that, a sceptical reader might ask? The same reader might go on to point out that she had already used a modified form of this device in a neglected, very engaging story called *The Man in the Brown Suit* (1924), although there it played only a minor part in the story. Perfectly true: but in *Roger Ackroyd* the device is at the heart of the book, which really could not exist without it. The whole thing is the blandest, most brilliant of deceptions. When we look back to see how it was done – well, as so often with Dame Agatha it is a matter of some assumptions that we are led to make because making them is customary, plus a few carefully chosen phrases intended to deceive without ever being positively untrue.

The trouble with plot devices is that they often obtrude, so that we have all plot and no story. Part of *Roger Ackroyd*'s triumphant success rests in the fact that the rest of the story is so perfectly typical of the period. A country squire is murdered, the body is found in the library, there is a butler and a housekeeper both of whom behave suspiciously, the cast of characters includes several with a motive for murder. All this, even in the middle Twenties, was far from new. The novelty rests in the fact that the murderer seems to fit so naturally into such a milieu, and yet truly does not belong to it at all. The plot device fits into the framework of the story as snugly as the pearl in its oyster.

One might feel that ingenuity in plot construction could hardly be taken further than *Roger Ackroyd*. Rather more than a decade after its publication, Dorothy L. Sayers suggested that the detective story as a pure puzzle was in gentle and painless decline, partly because those devices that had seemed so ingenious in the form's early days – the poisoned toothbrush, the evaporating ice dart, the pistol timed to fire when the grandfather clock in the library struck twelve – were worn out from too much use, and partly because readers' tastes had changed, so that they were increasingly asking for crime stories in which the characters were as important as the plot. She has proved a truthful prophet, although some of the crime story's developments would have surprised and displeased her. Agatha Christie's ingenuity, however, had always been verbal and visual rather than mechanical and scientific, and she responded to the idea that the detective puzzle was worn out by inventing new and still more dazzling conjuring tricks.

Are *The A.B.C. Murders* (1935) and *Ten Little Niggers* (1939) as good as *Roger Ackroyd*? Not quite, because the trick played on the reader is deliberately artificial rather than fitting naturally into the story. In the later books the Christie cleverness again leaves us gasping, but second and third readings show that the plot has been built around the device used, with total disregard for our belief in the story itself. Who can believe that those ten guilty people would in fact have accepted that mysterious invitation to stay on the small island in *Ten Little Niggers*? Who can believe in a murderer so reckless, and in a gull so stupid, as the characters in *The A.B.C. Murders*? Yet the books remain triumphs of ingenuity, and it is worth trying to see just how the tricks are done.

The A.B.C. Murders are apparently motiveless, or at least their motive seems to be purely alphabetical. Ascher is killed at Andover, Barnard at Bexhill and Clarke at Churston. A copy of an A.B.C. Railway Guide is placed beside the body, and each crime is announced beforehand in a taunting letter to Poirot. 'We're up against a homicidal maniac,' says one of the police investigators, but although Poirot agrees at the time, we know that this cannot be the case. There must be a logical answer.

That is the reader's assumption, and of course he is right. The problem is, then, how to maintain his interest through a series of crimes which in their details (I am trying not to give away too much) are for the most part irrelevant to the plot. This is managed by shifts of viewpoint from Hastings's first person narration to a third person view of the actions of a man named Alexander Bonaparte Cust, or A.B.C. Who is A.B.C.? He is always on the scene of the crime, and it seems that he must be the murderer. The presence of A.B.C. links what would otherwise appear disparate crimes in which we might lose interest. And another problem confronted the author, that of bringing together suspects involved in separate crimes and living in different parts of England. This too is managed with unobtrusive skill. The book is a masterwork of carefully concealed artifice.

And so is *Ten Little Niggers*. The way in which characters and plot are introduced has been described. At an early stage, then, we see what is going to happen. Some of these people are going to be killed, there will be a police investigation, and the person responsible will be discovered. But as death after death occurs, and no investigator appears, it is slowly borne in on us that the nursery rhyme ends with the line: 'And then there were none.' When only two people remain, one must be the murderer. It doesn't, however, work out like that. The book's last sentences embody the nature of the puzzle: 'When the sea goes down, there will come from the mainland boats and men. And they will find ten dead bodies and an unsolved problem on Indian Island.' Poirot does not appear in this book. How could he, when it is a problem that remains unsolved?

4

What are Agatha Christie's chances of survival as a writer who will be read a century from now? To a certain extent this depends upon the kind of society we live in. Although some of her books are published in the Soviet Union, it is unlikely that she would be much read in a Communist-ruled world. But if we approach the question in literary rather than social terms, will she be read in the year 2100, and if so, why?

To answer yes, as I would do, is not to say that she was a great or even a good writer, but rather to say that although the detective story is ephemeral literature, the puzzle which it embodies has a permanent appeal. Perhaps W. H. Auden was right in identifying the ideal detective story reader as one possessed by a sense of guilt, and in suggesting that detective stories should not be considered as art but as a kind of magic. Certainly its association with myth, and its links with the classical riddle, are strong. Few crime stories nowadays are detective novels – they belong, to vary what Auden said a little, to the real and not to an ideal world – and it is plausible to consider Dame Agatha Christie as the last notable figure of her kind. If her work survives it will be because she was the supreme mistress of a magical skill that is a permanent, although often secret, concern of humanity: the construction and the solution of puzzles.

Edmund Crispin

The Mistress of Simplicity
A conversation with H.R.F. Keating

KEATING: Agatha Christie is generally regarded as a superb plotter, but was her actual writing on the same level?

CRISPIN: I think not, no. She wrote dialogue very well – a lot of her books are dialogue almost entirely, with relatively little action – but I wouldn't say she was a particularly good stylist.

KEATING: No. So what was, if you like, unique about her work? Obviously it was enormously successful. What do you think is the key to that success?

CRISPIN: Oh, simplicity, I think, ultimately. Her plots, though in themselves often highly sophisticated, are rarely, if ever, sophisticated in their actual presentation: basic English words, relatively short sentences, relatively short paragraphs, minimal punctuation – these were her usual building-blocks. Incidentally, her simplicity helps her books to translate well, as does her lack of interest in police procedure, which naturally differs from country to country. In short, she is in some ways an ingenuous writer, so that she can be read happily not merely by Professors of Logic taking the train from Oxford to London but equally happily by children under the desk at school.

KEATING: Yes, but there have been other writers who have kept things fairly simple and certainly haven't been as successful artistically.

CRISPIN: Yes, that is so.

KEATING: What about, for instance, Erle Stanley Gardner, who was very successful and kept things even more simple?

CRISPIN: Though it's arguable that he overdid it, except perhaps in the A. A. Fair novels. The Perry Mason stories became not simple so much as simplistic, with constant repetition from page to page and from book to book of such clichés as 'The telephone rang. Della Street picked up the instrument.' Given character, plot and background, one feels that almost any of Gardner's secretaries could have written the book.

KEATING: Whereas Agatha Christie managed to avoid this sort of thing.

CRISPIN: Exactly. She had enough variety in her prose style to colour and alter the stereotyped form Erle Stanley Gardner used.

KEATING: And when you say variety, that's variety within books and variety from book to book?

CRISPIN: Yes, certainly, except that as regards single books the pace is rather even. Apart from that, there's variety within each book as well as between one book and another – much more variety than people realized when they bought a 'Christie for Christmas' on the vague assumption that it was all going to be the same mixture as before.

KEATING: Can you give an instance of the variety that she . . . ?

CRISPIN: Yes, certainly. *The Hollow*, for example – a story that hasn't a particularly good plot – is much more elaborately written than, say, *Death in the Clouds*.

KEATING: Or as Americans would say *Murder After Hours* is much more elaborate than *Death in the Air*. But her artistic success varied from book to book?

CRISPIN: Certainly it did, as with any other author. Though beyond a certain point people bought her anyway, because she was Agatha Christie and you just did buy the latest Agatha Christie. A sort of snowball effect.

KEATING: Is that quite fair? All over the world people bought, borrowed, begged or stole her books. Surely that can't have been entirely due to a snowball effect?

CRISPIN: No, you're right, of course. What they wanted from her, and what she could almost always provide, was 'escapism', a release, however temporary, from the anxieties of real life. The novelist E. M. Forster was once asked why he didn't face reality – to which he replied, 'How can I face reality when it's all round me?' And that's sound enough, you know. Most people, I fancy, have had the experience of seeming to be bedevilled from all directions at once.

KEATING: Would you say in fact that Agatha Christie made you face a tiny slice of reality in one direction?

CRISPIN: Yes. When one thinks of her, one thinks inevitably of English country life, rather than of English metropolitan life, and in particular of small villages and parsonages and possibly the Squire's large mansion, but not of factory towns, or coal mines, or any sort of commercialism.

KEATING: And yet she appealed to people who'd no idea of what an English village was like. Why do you think that was?

CRISPIN: Well, to a lesser extent because we are not, after all, the only nation to whom the exotic appeals. But to a much greater extent because the Christie characters were in many ways universal – so that an Icelander, for example, had no difficulty in recognizing his particular equivalent of Miss Marple in his Icelandic neighbour.

KEATING: Yes, I'm sure that there are Miss Marples all over the world. But not Poirots?

CRISPIN: Poirot – as opposed to Miss Marple – was a special case: an almost completely artificial conglomeration of trivial mannerisms. His creator, I might add, became very bored with him at quite an early stage in his career – whereas for Miss Marple she retained a certain affection to the last.

KEATING: So you'd say that she picked on the universal in human character – on the things we have in common rather than on the ways in which we differ – and that this was the aspect of us she brought to the fore?

CRISPIN: Yes. In several of her books she maintained that humanity was much the same all over the world; that its motives are the same whether you are Swedish, Hottentot or Chilean. Action, Agatha Christie either implies or specifically states, will provoke approximately the same reaction regardless of colour, creed or nationality.

KEATING: Now, you said earlier that her dialogue was good.

CRISPIN: Yes, I think it is. It runs very smoothly.

KEATING: And is it just a matter of smoothness? She had a good ear, presumably, for the way people speak in her circle.

CRISPIN: Yes, in her circle. But scarcely outside that circle. I can't remember her showing any command of dialect, for example, such as Gladys Mitchell excels at.

KEATING: You compare her with Gladys Mitchell. How does she compare with some of the other crime writers, for instance, with Ngaio Marsh?

CRISPIN: Well, Ngaio Marsh, I think, is a better stylist; but she can be very much duller, particularly in the middle of her books, with her detective Alleyn interviewing one suspect after another and getting nothing very relevant out of any of them. This can go on for a hundred pages or more and seems to me, personally, to be faulty construction, a fault almost completely absent from Agatha Christie.

KEATING: And she avoided this by being very aware of what her reader would want?

CRISPIN: True, but I think it was a sort of natural rather than an acquired craftsmanship. I think it would have bored her to have interview after interview after interview, *à la* Marsh.

KEATING: You mean that she had a temperamental instinct to write, rather than to write for either commercial or fashionable reasons?

CRISPIN: I think that's certainly true. And what interested her was not crime as such, but crime as . . . I suppose we have to call it intrigue. She did, as you know, write under the name of Mary Westmacott several straightforward romantic novels. But without her plot, her crime, to hang her story on, she seems to me to have been more or less lost.

KEATING: So it works out that she had an intense interest in her plot, and this kept her very strictly to her story.

CRISPIN: Yes. It kept her from irrelevance.

KEATING: In addition to which, it kept her from putting in things which other crime authors nowadays have made very familiar indeed.

CRISPIN: Yes. Things like detailed descriptions of sex and of violence. Even humour. She wasn't a humourless woman and there are occasional funny bits, such as the Mah Jongg game in *The Murder of Roger Ackroyd*. But even that she would have regarded as something of a distraction from the real business of the story, which was to enunciate a puzzle and solve it.

KEATING: So for this reason she left out sex and violence. Are there any other important omissions?

CRISPIN: Surprisingly many. Any serious discussion of politics or religion, for example, and also I think she was very seldom directly topical. Comfortable by the fire in the evening, you scarcely ever feel, as with so much crime fiction nowadays, that you're reading the morning papers with their settled gloom, their alarmist politics and so forth, yet a second time.

KEATING: Yes – although she did keep up-to-date in her settings. There's the lack of servants in the later books, in contrast for instance to their simply unstressed omnipresence in such a book as the last Miss Marple story, *Sleeping Murder*, which of course was written many years before she died. And in her eightieth book, *Passenger to Frankfurt*, there's even a passing reference to Marcuse.

CRISPIN: Oh, yes. She kept up with the times in so far as the smaller details of life were concerned. But I was thinking of larger things, the international issues and so forth. But domestic details are another matter. For one thing, she was interested in young people – and indeed the children in her books are often much more sharply individualized than the adults. But as far as the real-life ones were concerned, she shared in, and was mildly amused by, their special interests.

KEATING: Was this because of her large family of young relatives?

CRISPIN: Yes, it was rather a ramifying family. I never worked out who was who, but there was certainly a considerable number of them about the place. Not to mention dogs. Dogs and young people, they surrounded her. When I went to lunch, there would quite likely be sixteen people at table and a lot of them young people in whom she kept an interest. Like well brought-up children, they treated her with politeness but not with any special awe. She usually sat at the centre of the table, but they didn't show her any special deference just because she was Agatha Christie.

KEATING: To get back to things she left out, we haven't talked about her descriptive writing.

CRISPIN: Well, there was very little of that. As I was saying earlier, there wasn't much which wasn't dialogue. And also I think that, although she must have observed her surroundings, she very seldom uses an exotic setting in a documentary or detailed or convincing way. Someone would say 'Allah el Allah' or something, but that was just about as far as it would go. And she'd be aware that Jews don't eat pork and so forth. But I can't remember a description of any place, outside Britain, except possibly Petra. I think there was an extended description of Petra, the 'rose-red city – half as old as Time!'

KEATING: Could we find from that pile of books at your elbow some quite random examples of her customary method of describing principal settings for a book?

CRISPIN: Yes, of course. From *After the Funeral* (*Funerals Are Fatal* in America), 1953: 'Enderby Hall was a vast Victorian house built in the Gothic style.' And from *Dead Man's Folly*, 1956: 'They went on, down a steep hill through woods, then through big iron gates, and along a drive, winding up finally in front of a big white Georgian house looking out over a river.' Then in *Sleeping Murder*, 1976: 'Anstell Manor had a bleak aspect. It was a white house, set against a background of bleak hills. A winding drive led up through a dense shrubbery.' Quite adequate, but neither detailed nor atmospherically convincing.

KEATING: And what about her descriptions of people?

CRISPIN: She describes people very little. One has only the vaguest idea of what they look like.

KEATING: In *Sleeping Murder*, which I've just been reading, Miss Marple is described as being tall. Had you remembered her as tall?

Only rarely does Agatha Christie confer full physical descriptions on her characters. In the 1976 *Sleeping Murder*, Miss Marple is described as being *tall*, so belying the popular impression either of a small, busy woman, an impression perhaps brought about by her representation on stage by such as Barbara Mullen (*below on the left*), in *Murder at the Vicarage*, or of a large, double-chinned lady like Margaret Rutherford as the screen Miss Marple, in *Murder Ahoy* (*right*), and many others.

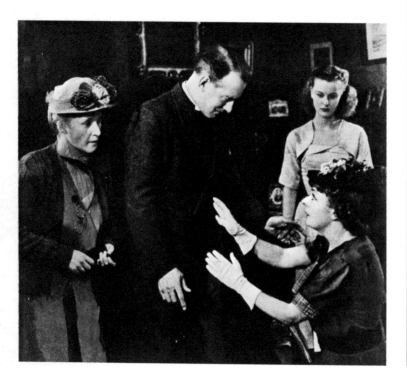

CRISPIN: No, I hadn't. I'd always thought of her as a little thing, knitting away busily or busy with the secateurs in the garden. So that came as quite a surprise.

KEATING: And could we find some examples of her descriptions of people, of main characters?

CRISPIN: In *Cards on the Table*, 1936, she wrote: 'Poirot had not previously met Colonel Race, but he knew something about him. A dark, handsome, deeply bronzed man of fifty, he was usually to be found in some outpost of empire – especially if there was trouble

brewing.' And then in *Curtain: Poirot's Last Case*, 1975: 'A frail elderly lady, with an abundance of curly white hair, pink cheeks, and a pair of cold pale blue eyes.' The last four words admittedly come as a mild shock, but the rest, I'm afraid, is little better than cliché.

KEATING: So, finally, is there one word which you might apply to explain the secret of the effect she had on readers?

CRISPIN: In saying 'one', Harry, I'm afraid you're being a bit over-optimistic. But I'll make it as short as I can. I think that a prime factor in Agatha Christie's success was tension created by cunning plot construction. Secondly, the plot was expressed as uncomplicatedly, and in as simple a prose, as was possible. Finally, one finds a curious satisfaction in what the Americans would call the 'desanitizing' of unpleasantness. In a Christie, you know, for example, that the corpse is not a real corpse, but merely the pretext for a puzzle. You know that the policeman is not a real policeman, but a good-natured dullard introduced on to the scene to emphasize the much greater intelligence of Poirot or Miss Marple. You know that there will be no loving description of the details of physical violence. You know (or up to a few years ago, used to know) that, although the murderer is going to be hanged, you will be kept well at a distance from this displeasing event. You know that although people may fall in love you will not be regaled with the physical details of what they do in bed. You know, relaxing with a Christie, that for an hour or two you can forget the authentic nastiness of life and submerge yourself in a world where, no matter how many murders may take place, you are essentially in never-never land. To paraphrase Forster, with reality all round you, you can close your eyes to it for a little while. And to do this, I believe, is psychologically healthy. It gives one a breathing space, a respite, a rest. When reality has once again to be coped with, we cope with it all the better for the break.

One writer who enables us to do this is Agatha Christie. We've discussed, a little, some of the techniques she uses in getting this particular effect. But there is no finally convincing explanation of how a middle-class woman, courteous and conventional and somewhat conformist in her ways, should so often have been able to weave the spell.

Michael Gilbert

A Very English Lady

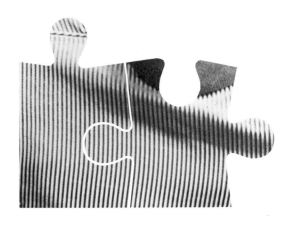

THE WRITERS of exciting books rarely seem to lead exciting lives. The adventurous conception, the interplay of characters, the crises, the tensions and the climaxes are locked up inside their own heads. As for real life that goes on its easy way, year follows year, each year marked by the milestone of another book or play.

A glance at the entry under 'Agatha Christie' in the 1975 edition of *Who's Who* suggests exactly this. It is not, of course, true. No one could have lived for eighty-five years, through two world wars, two marriages and a number of visits to the more deserted parts of the Middle East without encountering a fair measure of tragedy, comedy and romance.

Agatha Mary Clarissa Miller was born on 15 September 1890 at a house called Ashfield on the outskirts of Torquay. Her father was an American, Frederick Alvah Miller, a man in easy circumstances, whose income was said to be derived 'from a business in New York'. It was a business which seemed to flourish without any personal attention from him. The family group consisted of the mother, who was English, and to whom Agatha was devoted; a sister, Madge, and a brother, Monty, both older than her. Madge later wrote a number of books and turned the case of the Tichborne Claimant (a sensational Victorian imposture) into a play which was acted with success on the London stage.

This was the golden evening of the Victorian era. Mr Miller entertained his friends and neighbours and was patron of the Torquay Cricket Club. Life at Ashfield was a comfortable and undemanding round of social engagements. Mrs Miller sent Madge off to Roedean to absorb the traditional boarding-school education for girls. For Agatha, her ideas were different. Possibly she considered her an unsuitable subject for the rough and tumble of boarding school life. She was kept at home and taught by her mother and a succession of governesses.

Sir Max Mallowan, Agatha's second husband, whom I introduce here ahead of chronology, agrees that this lack of contact with other children may have contributed to making her unusually shy and introverted. He says: 'It is true that she had singing lessons in Paris and had considered becoming a professional opera singer, but her voice was not strong enough and she had reluctantly to abandon this intention. At one time, also, she considered becoming a concert pianist but her music master advised her that she was too nervous to consider playing in public concerts. Since a considerable measure of self-confidence was part of a professional player's equipment she abandoned her intention of playing professionally, but was a competent executant and practised seriously.'

A lot of pleasant things came to an end for a lot of people in 1914; among them the happy and self-sufficient family life of the Millers. 1914 was an important year for Agatha. She had been engaged for some time past to Archibald Christie, and married him in the summer of that year. He went straight off to the war, in the course of which he was to win the DSO and to receive the CMG. Agatha, after taking various first-aid courses, was accepted as a VAD nurse in the hospital which had been established in the Town Hall in Torquay. After two years there she moved into a dispensary. This may have been one of those climactic moments in a career which is not recognized at the time, but becomes clearly apparent in retrospect.

In his book, *Agatha Christie, Mistress of Mystery*, G. C. Ramsey quotes the remarkable poem, written by her at about this time, and published by Geoffrey Bles in 1925. It was called 'The Road of Dreams'. It is easy to see that it was with the eye of an artist, not of a doctor or a scientist, that this twenty-six-year-old woman looked at the bottles on the shelves of that Torquay dispensary.

> Here heavy syrups, thick and sweet
>   Prepared with skill and toil
> And there, distilled in precious drops
>   Stand many a spiced oil
> Lavender, Nutmeg and Sandalwood
>   Cinnamon, Clove and Pine,
> While above, in palest primrose hue
>   The Flowers of Sulphur shine.

And then:

> High on the wall, beneath Lock and Key
>   The powers of the Quick and the Dead
> Little low bottles of blue and green
>   Each with a legend red
> In the depths beneath their slender necks
>   There is Romance and to spare
> *Oh, who shall say where Romance is?*
> *If Romance is not here.*

Where, if not in that dispensary, in 1916, when an idea was already germinating in Agatha's mind? It was going to be a most mysterious affair. It was going to involve the use, or misuse, of poisons. It was going to feature a detective with distinctive characteristics, a stage Frenchman – or perhaps a Belgian, in honour of the Belgian refugees who had come to Torquay in 1914.

There is a story that Agatha was provoked into writing by some remark made by her sister, but to attach any importance to this is to confuse the occasion and the cause. People do not undertake the labour of writing because of some casual remark made by a friend.

'The brilliant writer of detective stories',
The Sketch enthused in 1924, picturing
her in her Sunningdale home and
promising 'a new series of stories
by the same writer'.

They undertake it because of what is already inside their heads, screaming to be let out.

It was to be four years, and six publishers later, before *The Mysterious Affair at Styles* eventually saw the light of day in 1920 over the imprint of John Lane of the Bodley Head.

(In parenthesis, who *were* those six publishers who turned it down? One of them, if one can believe a comment made by Agatha to Sir Max, was Heinemann. Who were the other five? And how on earth could they have rejected this particular manuscript? Perhaps they didn't bother to read it?)

The years after the war started happily enough. Colonel Christie was home from France, his honours thick upon him. A house was bought and named 'Styles' after the first novel. In 1919 a daughter, Rosalind, was born. Further books appeared; two of them were what were just beginning to be called 'Who-dunnits'; two were thrillers; and one was a collection of short stories; the latter a traditional ragbag of Missing Wills, Veiled Ladies, Million Dollar Robberies and a Kidnapped Prime Minister (presumably a blend of Mr Asquith and Mr Lloyd George).

Underneath, things were not going smoothly. It was a mixed-up time of success and unhappiness.

On the success side of the balance sheet stood *The Murder of Roger Ackroyd*. This has long been accepted as one of the finest of Agatha's detective stories. There was an element of leg-pull about it, but it was a scrupulously fair leg-pull. As Dorothy L. Sayers commented, the only people who complained that the book was unfair were people who had been booby-trapped by it.

It was an immediate and unqualified success. It received the compliment, rare with a detective story, of being serialized in the *Daily News*. It made Agatha's name known to a wide circle of readers and ensured that her next books would be welcomed and discussed.

(My mother, who was an avid reader of who-dunnits, but perennially hard-up, scraped together the money to buy a first edition, which I still possess. We took it with us on a holiday to Belgium that August and I identified four different characters, with confidence, as the murderer; in each case incorrectly.)

At 'Styles', there was trouble. Differences had been developing between Agatha and Colonel Christie. It may have been the fault of neither side. There must have been a lot of marriages broken up by four years' enforced separation of the husband at the front and the corresponding immersion of the wife in her own life and her own work. Whatever the reason, things came to a head in December of 1926.

Colonel Christie had formed an attachment for a Miss Neele, who lived at Godalming. On the morning of 4 December he took advantage of Agatha's absence from the house, packed his bags and left for Miss Neele's house. When Agatha got back the news was broken to her by her secretary. At nine o'clock that night she got out the car, which she had recently learned to handle, and drove off. The secretary telephoned Colonel Christie, who came back in a hurry.

The next known fact is that George Best, a fifteen-year-old gipsy lad, found the car toppled over an embankment near the Silent Pool at Newlands Corner on the Surrey escarpment.

It was as though someone had pressed a button which released an astonishing outpouring of publicity. Reading the pages of the newspapers which came out in the next few days, one is staggered by the importance attached by the press to this event. Banner headlines span two and three columns of print. Every day brings a 'development'. Eminent public characters comment and speculate.

On 7 December the *Daily News* offered a reward of £100 for information. When Colonel Christie's attention was drawn to it, he said: 'I would gladly give £500 if I could only hear where my wife is.' He added, disingenuously, that he had been away for the weekend and was not at home when his wife's disappearance was reported. The *Daily News*, exercising its prerogative of innuendo, added: 'The fact that she was not wearing a wedding ring at the time of her disappearance is considered to be of no special significance.'

On 8 December a local chemist, a Mr Gilling, revealed that Agatha had often discussed with him different methods of committing suicide, and a Mrs Kitching came forward and created some excitement by saying that she had seen a woman at midday on that Saturday walking in a dazed fashion near Albury. She had never met Agatha, but identified her positively from photographs published in the press. On the following day a woman's right-foot patent-leather shoe was found.

On 10 December Colonel Christie, who was being harried by the press, scouted the suggestion of suicide, and put forward, for the first time, an unkind suggestion which was to acquire currency as

£100 REWARD.

A new photograph of Mrs. Christie.

The "Daily News" offers £100 reward to the first person furnishing us with first information leading to the discovery of the whereabouts, if alive, of Mrs. Christie.

Information should be telephoned to the "Daily News" (Telephone : Central 5000', or telegraphed, or conveyed by a personal call at the "Daily News" Office, 19, Bouverie-street, E.C 4.

HOW TO RECOGNISE HER.

Age	35
Height	5ft. 7in.
Figure	Well-built.
Hair	Reddish and shingled.
Eyes	Grey.
Complexion	Fair.

WEARING :

Green jumper.
Green velour hat.
Platinum ring with one pearl.
Probably carrying a black handbag.

SHOE AND SCARF

FOUND ON DOWNS YESTERDAY.

A woman's patent shoe.
A woman's scarf.

These articles, found by searchers for Mrs. Agatha Christie, the missing novelist, on the Downs near Guildford yesterday, have led the police to organise an intensified search, in which 500 men will take part to-day.

The shoe resembles those Mrs. Christie is believed to have been wearing. It was found about 50 yards down the hillside from Newlands Corner, where the novelist's car was abandoned.

A police guard has been posted outside The Styles, the home of Colonel and Mrs. Christie—at the Colonel's request, he states.

A full report of yesterday's developments appears on Page Five.

The lady vanishes : in the vanguard of the hunt for the missing author was the *Daily News*, which offered £100 reward for information. Her subsequent reappearance at a Harrogate hotel led to the paper sending a piqued telegram requesting an 'authentic explanation' from the writer.
Right : Colonel Christie, the novelist's first husband, and 'Styles', their Berkshire home, named after her first novel and itself now the setting for a mysterious affair.
Below right : Speculation by the *Daily News* on possible disguises assumed by the runaway author.

Overleaf : Hundreds of policemen, not to mention thousands of enthusiastic amateurs, were involved in the search.
Top : Police reconstruct the scene of the mystery around the abandoned car in which Agatha Christie had left 'Styles'.
Below : Police beaters scour the nearby countryside for clues.
Opposite : Excited crowds gather at King's Cross station to greet the train on which the Christies returned from Harrogate to London.

MRS. CHRISTIE DISGUISED.

Mrs. Agatha Christie as she was last seen (centre), and (on left and right) how she may have disguised herself by altering the style of her hairdressing and by wearing glasses. Col. Christie says his wife had stated that she could disappear at will if she liked, and, in view of the fact that she was a writer of detective stories, it would be very natural for her to adopt some form of disguise to carry out that idea.

time went on. He told the *Daily News*, which was leading the hunt:
'My wife said to me, some time ago, that she could disappear at will
and would defy anyone to find her. This shows that the possibility of
engineering her disappearance was running through her mind.'

Next day a powder puff was found, in a lonely hut. This was
handed over to a clairvoyant who said that the body of its owner
would be found in a log house. The hint was taken, and a log house
was quickly discovered, but disappointingly no body in it.

Edgar Wallace, whose play *The Ringer* was pulling in the audiences
at Wyndhams Theatre, declared that what had happened was a
typical example of mental reprisal. He said: 'Her intention seems to
have been to spite an unknown person who would be distressed by
her disappearance.' The readers of the *Daily Mail*, in which this
comment appeared, cannot have had much difficulty in identifying
the person referred to.

By the weekend the search had escalated into the realms of fantasy.
Hundreds of policemen, thousands of enthusiastic amateurs, Scouts,

dogs, aeroplanes, diviners and divers were scouring the countryside and the pools for clues and propounding theories for the press.

Then, quite suddenly, it all stopped. On 13 December a member of the staff of the Hydro Hotel at Harrogate claimed the £100 reward. He said that Agatha had been staying there for nine days, having arrived in a taxi-cab after lunch on the previous Saturday. The other guests at the hotel, who had been charmed by Agatha's manner, all agreed that she was obviously suffering from loss of memory. The whole of her actions, they said, had been so perfectly normal that this was the only possible explanation.

The press, who were feeling piqued, were not so certain. The *Daily News* sent (and published) a telegram: 'In view wide-spread criticism your disappearance strongly urge desirability authentic explanation from yourself to thousands of public who joined in costly search and cannot understand your loss of memory theory.'

Colonel Christie, who had hurried to Harrogate, said that neither he nor his wife were making any further statements.

What was really behind it?

A good and balanced account of the episode was written recently for the *New Statesman* by Ritchie Calder. Unlike many commentators he did know what he was talking about, having been himself engaged in the search as a very junior reporter on the staff of the *Daily News*. He says: 'In retrospect, it is difficult to decide who were most responsible, the police or the press, for a "missing person" enquiry being blown up into the sensation of the century.' This seems a just verdict.

Let us put the last word into the mouth of Hercule Poirot: 'You are suggesting, my dear Hastings, that it was what you might term a publicity stunt. Yes? But consider two points. First that the lady had, by that time, not the slightest need for publicity. She had a full measure of it already. Secondly a more important point, which must always be considered in matters of this sort. The known character of the suspect. Can you really visualize a lady of genuine modesty, with a retiring disposition and an extreme dislike of public intervention in her affairs deliberately making herself the centre of a *cause célèbre* and bringing down on herself the country-wide attention of the sensational press. If you have no better solution to offer than that, *mon cher* Hastings, I suggest that you keep silent.'

Hastings retires, abashed.

Life gradually resumed its routine. The divorce, which followed not long after, revived a flicker of interest. Then writing was resumed.

In 1927 there was a thriller. In 1928 a who-dunnit, in 1929 a thriller again, *The Seven Dials Mystery*, and in the same year a reappearance of that happy-go-lucky pair Tommy and Tuppence as *Partners in Crime*.

The clouds were lifting and Agatha decided that a holiday would be in order. After much thought and careful discussions with a helpful travel agent she selected the West Indies as her destination. Tickets were bought and reservations were made. Then, at the eleventh hour, she changed her mind. She announced that she would go to Baghdad.

Agatha was normally punctilious about honouring obligations and carrying out plans. Why did she make such an uncharacteristic gesture? She met someone who enchanted her with his account of Baghdad, the River Tigris and the ancient cities being excavated thereabouts. The travel agent took it badly, but rallied round. All arrangements were changed. She went to Baghdad. To punish her for her wilfulness fate here threw her into the company of 'a lobster of a woman'. (She was to reappear in many novels.) To escape her claws, Agatha presumed on a slight acquaintance with Sir Leonard Woolley who was in charge of the joint British Museum and Museum of the University of Pennsylvania Expedition to Ur of the Chaldees.

Sir Leonard Woolley's wife, Lady Katharine, found Agatha agreeable company. Not only was she accorded the unusual honour of being invited to remain with the digging team, but she was urged to join them again in the following year. She accepted, and it was then that she met Max Mallowan, one of the Archaeologist Assistants on the Woolleys' staff who had been away on the previous occasion having his appendix removed. When the digging season of 1929–30 was nearly over, in March, Lady Woolley decreed that Max should conduct Agatha back to England on the Orient Express. Lady Woolley's decrees were never questioned. The pair departed. In September of that same year they were married.

Having allowed Max to sneak into the story by a side door, it is now time to introduce him formally.

He was born in London in 1904, educated at Lancing and New College, Oxford, and his assignment at Ur of the Chaldees was the first of the countless archaeological expeditions and excavations

Sir Leonard Woolley (*below*), was in charge of the 1929 expedition to excavate the tombs of Ur in Iraq. His invitation to Agatha Christie to rejoin the group the following year was to prove a turning-point in her life, for it was then that she met Max Mallowan (in the centre of the archaeological dig, *right*), one of the Assistants on Woolley's staff. Mallowan conducted his future wife back to England in the Orient Express.

which have led him steadily to the top of his chosen profession. He is a fellow of All Souls, a Professor Emeritus of Western Asiatic Archaeology in the University of London, a Trustee of the British Museum, the author of half a dozen books and of numerous articles in newspapers and learned journals and the holder of enough chairmanships, presidencies, editorships, lectureships, medals and memberships of learned bodies, British and foreign, to fill twenty closely printed lines in *Who's Who*. He was knighted in 1968.

At the point at which we left him, he was a young archaeologist, busy setting up house in Sheffield Terrace, Kensington. Agatha decorated the whole interior with enthusiasm and taste and established a music room for herself on the top floor.

It was not long before a joint digging and writing venture was

Below right : 'Abram's Mound' before its excavation, the subject of Woolley's expedition.

NOVELIST ON THRILLING TRIP

Agatha Christie and a Lost People

IRAQ SEARCH

In an effort to discover a lost civilisation, believed to have existed for some hundreds of years in Northern Iraq over 6,000 years ago, an expedition under the auspices of the British Museum is leaving London to-day.

The expedition will be under the direction of Mr. M. E. Mallowan, who assisted Dr. Campbell Thompson in last year's excavations at Nineveh. Mr. Mallowan's wife, Agatha Christie, the well-known novelist, is accompanying the expedition.

Sir Edgar Bonham-Carter, chairman of the Executive Committee of the British School of Archæology in Iraq, said yesterday:—

Agatha Christie.

"The expedition is to excavate a prehistoric site at Arpachiyah, near Nineveh, where it is hoped to find evidence of a lost civilisation which existed before the rise of Ur. We confidently expect that Arpachiyah will reveal evidence of that early civilisation in Mesopotamia.

"Dr. Campbell Thompson's work last year revealed relics of a prehistoric people who were skilled in the making of decorative pottery.

"Similar pottery has been found among the mounds near Arpachiyah. We do not know whether great architectural remains are also to be found.

"In one of the mounds of Northern Iraq evidence has been found of habitation over 6,000 years ago, and Mr. Mallowan's expedition will attempt to gain further knowledge of these ancient people and their work."

planned. By 1935 Max was no longer an assistant. He was in charge. First, in 1933, at Arpachiyah. Then, between 1934 and 1936, at Chagar Bazar and Brak in Syria. It is at this point that we reach the only full-length piece of autobiography published in Agatha's lifetime. She called it 'an inconsequent chronicle', an answer to the question which cropped up so often. 'So you dig in Syria? Do tell me about it. How do you live? In a tent?'

'Most people', she says, 'probably do not want to know. It is just the small change of conversation. But there are, now and then, one or two people who are really interested.'

The book was started before the war, finished in 1944, published in 1946 and revised and reprinted in 1975. It must have been one of the last volumes that Agatha saw. I suspect that it was her favourite.

The title, *Come, Tell Me How You Live*, is taken from the piece of light verse which prefaces the book. It is a dedication, in rhyme, to Max. (A 'tell', by the way, is a bump in the earth which may, when investigated, produce archaeological treasure trove; or, equally often, may not.)

> I'll tell you everything I can
>   If you will listen well
> I met an erudite young man
>   A-sitting on a Tell
> 'Who are you, sir?' to him I said
>   'For what is it you look?'
> His answer trickled through my head
>   Like bloodstains in a book.
>
> He said, 'I look for aged pots
>   Of prehistoric days,
> And then I measure them in lots
>   And lots of different ways.
> And then (like you) I start to write,
>   My words are twice as long
> As yours, and far more erudite
>   They prove my colleagues wrong.
> But I was thinking of a plan
>   To kill a millionaire
> And hide the body in a van
>   Or some large Frigidaire –

And so on, through eight or nine verses parodying Lewis Carroll, dedicated to the memory

Left By 1933 Max Mallowan was no longer an assistant but in charge of the expedition to the prehistoric site of Arpachiyah. His wife accompanied him on what were to become joint digging and writing ventures. Contemporary newspapers needed little persuasion to seize upon the project's romantic possibilities.

Of that young man I used to know
  Whose thoughts were in the long ago
Whose pockets sagged with potsherds so
  Who lectured learnedly and low,
Who used long words I didn't know
  Whose eyes, with fervour all aglow
Upon the ground looked to and fro
  Who sought conclusively to show
That there were things I ought to know
  And that with him I ought to go
And dig upon a Tell.

It is a delightful book, full of the pleasure of youth re-found at the age of forty; of a new life to live; a mixture of ancient pots and modern plots; of friends known by nicknames and a solitary skull which was named Lord Edgware in advance of the book in which the peer of that name dies.

We also pick up some rare, but very human, references to Agatha's family. Her mother who, thrilled by the novelty of the zip fastener, had a pair of corsets specially made for her which zipped up in front. 'The results were unfortunate in the extreme. Not only was the zipping up fraught with agony, but the corsets then obstinately refused to de-zip. Owing to my mother's Victorian modesty it seemed possible that she would remain in those corsets for the remainder of her life. A woman in the Iron Corset.'

There is a glimpse too of her sister Madge, coming to see the party off from Victoria: 'My sister says tearfully that she has a feeling that she will never see me again. I am not very much impressed, because she has felt this every time I go to the East. And what, she asks, is she to do if Rosalind gets appendicitis? There seems no reason why my fourteen-year-old daughter should get appendicitis and all I can think of to reply is, "Don't operate on her yourself!" For my sister has a reputation for hasty action with her scissors, attacking impartially boils, haircutting, and dress-making – usually, I must admit, with great success.'

The accepted period for Middle East digging, in those more spacious pre-war days, was from October to March and the book deals, in detail, with two such digs, in the years 1935–6 and 1936–7, at Chagar Bazar and at Brak. They were uneasy years in England, with Hitler and Mussolini strutting before their troops in Europe,

Coming to Baghdad: the Mallowans about to fly to Baghdad
in 1950 for further archaeological excavations. Much of
Agatha Christie's writing was done on these expeditions
('Splendid conditions. No telephone'), and in this instance
They Came to Baghdad was published in the following year.

and our own Abdication crisis at home. In a remote region of Syria, they passed very happily.

The 'family' was increased by the advent of 'The Colonel', 'Bumps', and 'Mac'. The Colonel was Colonel Alec Burn, of the Indian Army, a friend of the Mallowans both on excavations in the Middle East and at home, where he and Agatha used to explore old London together. He was a keen amateur archaeologist, with a sense of humour, a man for all seasons. Bumps, who joined the party for the second dig, was a young architect. His nickname arose out of an incautious remark made by him to the Colonel in the train on their journey out. In the early dawn, as they were approaching their destination, he pulled up the blind, and gazed with interest at the country where the next few months of his life were to be spent. 'Curious place this,' he remarks. 'It's all over bumps.' 'Bumps, indeed,' cried the Colonel. 'Don't you realize that each of those bumps is a buried city, dating back thousands of years.' Mac, another young architect, was the son of Sir George Macartney, who was, for over thirty years, Consul-General in Kashgar. Despite the fact that Mac hardly opened his mouth unless directly provoked, and seemed, at first blush, to be totally lacking in any sense of humour, he was quite clearly one of Agatha's favourite characters.

'Fleas and bugs don't bite him,' she tells an incredulous Bumps. 'He doesn't mind what he sleeps on. He never seems to have any luggage or personal possessions. Just his plaid rug and his diary.'

The interaction of these disparate characters was observed by Agatha with a novelist's eye.

The Good Samaritan story has a reality here which it cannot have among crowded streets, police, ambulances, hospitals and public assistance. If a man fell by the wayside on the broad desert track from Hasetshe to Der-ez-zor the story could easily happen today and it illustrates the enormous value which compassion has in the eyes of desert folk.

'How many of us,' Max asks suddenly, 'would really succour another human being in conditions where there were no witnesses, no force of public opinion, no knowledge or censure of a failure to extend aid?'

'Everyone, of course,' says the Colonel firmly.

'No, but would they?' persists Max. 'A man is lying there, dying. Death is not very important here. You are in a hurry. You have business to do. You do not want delay or bother. The man is nothing whatever to you. And nobody will ever know –'

We all sit back and think, and we are all, I think, a little shattered. Are we so sure, after all, of our essential humanity?

After a long pause Bumps says slowly, 'I *think* I would . . . Yes, I think I would. I might go on, and then, perhaps feel ashamed and come back.'

The Colonel agrees.

'Just so. One wouldn't feel comfortable.'

Max says he thinks so, too, but he isn't nearly so sure about himself as he would like to be, and I concur with him.

We all sit silent for a while, and then I realise that, as usual Mac has made no contribution.

'What would you do, Mac?'

Mac starts slightly, coming out of a pleasant abstraction.

'Me?' His tone is surprised. 'Oh, I would go on. I wouldn't stop.'

We all look interestedly at Mac, who shakes his head.

'People die so much out here. One feels that a little sooner or later doesn't matter. I really wouldn't expect anyone to stop for *me*.'

No, that is true. Mac wouldn't.

His gentle voice goes on. 'It is much better, I think, to go straight on with what one is doing, without being continually deflected by outside people and happenings.'

Our interested gaze persists. Suddenly an idea strikes me.

'But suppose, Mac,' I say, 'that it was a horse?'

'Oh, a horse,' says Mac, becoming quite human and alive, and not remote at all. 'That would be quite different, of course. I'd do everything I possibly could for a horse.'

'This is not a profound book,' says the authoress in the foreword. 'It will give you no interesting side-lights on archaeology, there will be no beautiful descriptions of scenery, no treating of economic problems, no racial reflections, no history.'

Perhaps not, but there is something even more valuable. The real Agatha Christie, so carefully concealed behind the formal list of novels in *Who's Who*, behind the façade of the novels themselves, behind the very occasional anecdote, peeps out, for me, from the pages of this one book, begun before the war, laid aside, and completed among the sirens and the searchlights and the shortages and the dangers of wartime London.

A chronicle of small beer maybe, but when other vintages are turning sour small beer can be very refreshing.

'Writing this simple record has been not a task but a labour of love. For I love that gentle, fertile country and its simple people, who know

how to laugh and how to enjoy life; who are idle and gay, and who have dignity, good manners and a great sense of humour, and to whom death is not terrible.'

The war had separated husband and wife. Max had joined the RAFVR and had been posted with the rank of Wing Commander to Allied Headquarters, Middle East, as an adviser on Arab Affairs. He later became Secretary of Arab Affairs at Tripoli, and ultimately Deputy Chief Secretary for Western Libya.

Agatha, meanwhile, went on writing and working. She got a job as a VAD dispenser at University College Hospital in London and re-familiarized herself in practice with some of the drugs and poisons which she had been using in fiction. Her knowledge of them was, by this time, far from superficial. Martindale's *Extra Pharmacopoeia* was

During the Second World War, Agatha
Christie worked as a hospital dispenser,
as she had done in the 1914–18 war, this
time at University College Hospital,
London (*left*), where she may have
encountered some of the drugs and
poisons which she was to use in her
fiction – the 1945 *Sparkling Cyanide*
for example. Her pre-eminence was
challenged at this time only by
Margery Allingham (*below*) and
Dorothy L. Sayers (*right*).

one of the most studied books in what had become a considerable
medico-legal library in the flat she had taken for the duration of the
war in Lawn Road, Hampstead.

'No horrific experiences,' says Max, 'but, like other Londoners,
she was continuously being chased by flying bombs when she returned
home from work at the hospital.' Work was the anodyne. It was a
good time for writing (if you could distract your mind from noises
off). There was little else to do in the evenings.

The war years produced twelve completed novels, among them
some of her best known, such as the fantastically ingenious *Ten Little
Niggers* (given various titles in America) and *Sparkling Cyanide* (in
America *Remembered Death*). Most of them are who-dunnits in traditional form, but in one of them (*N or M?*) we have the indomitable,

The recipe for success? Agatha Christie in the kitchen (*above*)
of Greenway House, and (*right*) referring to one of her large collection
of books, *The Body in the Library* perhaps!

The Mallowans bought Greenway House, standing on the upper
reaches of the River Dart, as a holiday home in 1939.
These pictures, taken in 1946, show the couple together
at the boat-house (*left*), and in the study.

and ageless, Tommy and Tuppence dealing with Fifth Columnists and spies. There were also three plays: a dramatization of *Ten Little Niggers*, *Peril at End House* and *Appointment with Death*; and one of the six straight novels which she wrote under the name of Mary Westmacott dates from this period.

This was a remarkable output for an authoress who was working long hours at the hospital, and was faced with the problem, which many Londoners will remember, of getting to and from her work, through the shattered streets of a blacked-out city. The normal shortages affected her very little. She was a non-smoker and a non-drinker. Max had done his best about this, and every alcoholic drink from wine and whisky up to vodka and rum had been dutifully sampled by Agatha and successively rejected. They simply did not appeal.

When Max came back, they gave up the wartime flat and went off to their house at 22 Cresswell Place, South Kensington, and the pre-war routine was gradually resumed. In 1947 and 1949 there were expeditions to Nimrud, the ancient military capital of Assyria, and in the Tigris Valley. The wartime spate of writing was reduced to a steady stream, much of it done on these expeditions. ('Splendid conditions. No telephone.') Every year from 1947 onwards produced its novel. At first she was one of three queens of crime-writing. After Dorothy L. Sayers and Margery Allingham died, she reigned alone, in undisputed pre-eminence. She was no longer merely well known. She was famous. Her books were translated into almost every spoken language. Her world sales were reckoned to be more than three hundred million.

It was not her books, however, which put the cap-stone on her triumphal arch. In 1947 Queen Mary, who was a Christie fan, asked her to try her hand at a radio play. A royal request is a command. Agatha wrote a forty-five minute radio play, based on an idea which she had been saving up for a short story. As far as could be judged from the reactions of a radio audience it seemed to be effective. Queen Mary liked it. Agatha decided to elaborate it and turn it into a stage play. It was called *The Mousetrap*, and was produced at the Ambassadors Theatre, in 1952.

It is still running, having overtaken, broken and annihilated every previous record for a continuous theatrical run anywhere in the world.

A rare picture of Agatha Christie with
Sir Max Mallowan in the last months of her life,
when her public appearances, never frequent,
had almost ceased entirely.

Others will analyse the reasons for this staggering success. Its effects on Agatha were minimal. She came to consider it 'not a bad play' but it was not the one she liked best. Her favourite, beyond question, was *Witness for the Prosecution*. Most critics agreed with this choice. It is commonly said that an intricate 'who-dunnit', which depends for its effect on a surprise revelation in the last chapter, will never succeed on the stage, since by that point the audience will be furtively collecting their coats and handbags and worrying not about the identity of the murderer but about the time of the last train home. One can only record that the theatrical ingenuity of the last minutes of *Witness for the Prosecution* kept the most restive members of the audience nailed to their seats. On the first night, at the Winter Garden Theatre, a unique and spontaneous tribute was paid. The whole cast lined the front of the stage and bowed to the box where the authoress was seated.

The financial rewards of *The Mousetrap* meant nothing to Agatha. She had more income from her books than she could reasonably use. A major proportion of it had, in any event, to be handed straight back to the Revenue. By this time her way of life was settled. She and Max had two houses, Greenway House, on the upper reaches of the River Dart, in Devonshire, which they had bought as a holiday house in 1939, and Winterbrook House near Oxford. There were occasional visits to London to see her agents, Hughes Massie, or for the annual dinners of the Detection Club and other private functions. Public appearances were out. If she could not refuse to make a speech at some local function, she stipulated that it should not be longer than two minutes (an admirable rule that others might follow).

Inevitably there were honours. An honorary Doctorate of Literature, and the CBE in 1956. Finally, in 1971, she was made a Dame of the British Empire.

Life went on, peacefully and happily. Rosalind had married and there was a grandson and in due course great-grandchildren; and more plays; and a book every year, in time for the Christmas market. Until, in the end, death came, at the last, for this very English lady on 12 January 1976.

Emma Lathen

Cornwallis's Revenge

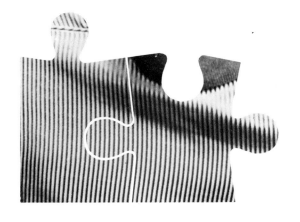

IN 1781 LORD CORNWALLIS surrendered to George Washington at Yorktown and, for all practical purposes, the Revolutionary War was over. The viscount went on to a distinguished career in India, the rebels became preoccupied with the problems of forging a new political state, and the world assumed that British dominion over the colonies was at an end. There the matter rested until 1920 which saw the publication of the first American edition of *The Mysterious Affair at Styles*. Now, fifty-six years later, any detached observer on these shores would have to admit that the second British Expeditionary Force has been considerably more successful than the first.

The invasion, of course, has not gone unresisted. Powerful troops with a knowledge of the terrain have tried to stem the tide. For instance, all across America in big cities and small towns, there are Christian Science Reading Rooms stocked with inspirational and uplifting literature. *Science and Health* is on every table. *Das Kapital* is not available and neither is *The Murder of Roger Ackroyd*. Similarly, the indefatigable Gideon Society optimistically equips all our motel rooms with a Holy Bible. Tourists wishing to read *Imperialism* or *The A.B.C. Murders* must provide their own copies. And so it goes. Utah, the 'Sagebrush State', is virtually blanketed with The Book of Mormon.

With such forces at their disposal it is small wonder that, purely as authors, Mary Baker Eddy *et al.* have beaten Karl Marx and V. I. Lenin hands down over here. But they haven't made a dent in Agatha Christie. Without divine intercession – or coercive methods of distribution – Dame Agatha has achieved Napoleonic triumphs which her publishers persistently and vainly attempt to describe: forty-eight million hardback Christies sold since 1923 (Alaska and Hawaii not included), 200 million (or is it billion?) paperbacks. Then there are book club sales, triple deckers, boxed gift sets and more short stories than O. Henry, Ernest Hemingway, and Damon Runyon combined. When sales figures no longer have any meaning, evocative collateral details are produced:

1. A column composed of all US editions of *Peril at End House* would stretch from Peoria, Illinois, to the moon.

2. Merely keeping *What Mrs McGillicuddy Saw!* in print in the United States deforests five thousand woodland acres in Maine every year (and in England it's being kept in print as *4.50 From Paddington*).

3. Of all departing passengers on United Airlines – going anywhere

– 58.6 per cent carry hand luggage and 47.2 per cent carry an Agatha Christie.

Naturally statistics like these awe publishers, agents and even critics. Nevertheless, they are not the best way to take Agatha Christie's transatlantic measure. For that Herculean task, books published, sold, borrowed and stolen are irrelevant. Population trends are the only reliable index. The more Americans there are, the more people there are reading *The Body in the Library*. It is that simple. Agatha Christie has become an integral element of the American way of life, and there are demographic studies to prove it.

Consider childhood as an example. There are over nine million pre-schoolers in these fifty states. Fragmentary data suggest that as many as 17.4 per cent of them are read to sleep by parents. Is Mother Goose likely to be meaningful to the modern toddler, let alone his mother and father? No, far more consonant with life styles from New York to California is:

THE MURDER OF ROGER ACKROYD
RETOLD BY GEORGE WEAR
Tales Retold for Easy Reading
Oxford University Press, 1948

When these infants leave the nest they very soon learn that Agatha Christie occupies an important place in the process of educating responsible citizens of the Republic. Having mastered the alphabet (A is for Arsenic, B is for Belladonna . . .?), they are now ready to enter the world of literature under their own steam. And there, waiting for them, is a student edition of *And Then There Were None* (edited by Harry Shefter *et al.*, Washington Square Press). Gone are David Copperfield, Silas Marner and, for that matter, Holden Caulfield. The future belongs to Hercule Poirot.

After secondary school comes college. And in many a curriculum Agatha Christie is a recognized discipline, comparable to social psychology or thermal dynamics. The aspiring undergraduate can start with an introductory survey, *The Modern Mystery Novel from S. S. Van Dine to A. Christie*, move on through more specialized courses, and finally proceed to a research seminar. If he has been sufficiently diligent, the fruits of his labours may appear in *The Journal of Popular Culture*, Bowling Green University, Bowling Green, Ohio.

In a world teeming with improbable statistics, it still requires fortitude to admit that, of all Americans between the ages of three and thirty-four, over sixty-one million (53.6 per cent) are attending school in some fashion. This percentage tells its own tale of thousands of postgraduates jostling for a little plot of virgin scholarship to call their own. Gone are the days when there existed a single flower in Proust, a single musical motif in Thomas Mann, that had not been analysed to smithereens. Inexorably the horde has advanced on the last frontier. To date the results have been disappointing. America still awaits a seminal work rivalling Sweden's contribution to modern linguistics:

Frank Behre, *Studies in Agatha Christie's Writings : The Behavior of 'a good (great) deal, a lot, lots, much, plenty, many, a good (great) many'*, Goteborg Universitet, 1967.

There are no reliable data for consideration of Agatha Christie in the summer school or in adult education. It should be noted, however, that the Evelyn Wood Institute of Speed Reading does not lag behind other renowned institutions of learning. 'Agatha Christie', declared a well-informed source, 'is one of the few authors guaranteed to help students break the lip-moving habit.'

But schooldays are the least of it. Agatha Christie is part and parcel of real life in the US, in sickness and in health, in good times and bad. Two million Americans are currently in health-related institutions. At any given moment of the day it is safe to say that half of them are either having their temperature taken or reading an Agatha Christie. The librarian at a veterans' hospital in the Midwest reports her 384 assorted Christies wear out faster than they can be replaced. The bookstore of a prominent New England teaching hospital stocks a hundred titles, of which forty-five are Christies – and always will be. At Boston's famous Lying-In Hospital it would be an adventurous friend who appeared during visiting hours bearing anything but an Agatha Christie. Mothers of twins probably expect two.

In the long twilight of life as well, our 22,431,000 senior citizens lean heavily on Agatha Christie. For the elderly confined to nursing and convalescent homes, she is more than a prop. She is a necessity. Says the specialist charged with bookmobile deliveries in the Denver area: 'I put Agatha Christie right up there with Medicare, Medicaid and Social Security in making old age tolerable.'

Even before the golden years, Agatha Christie comforts the unfortunate. In every year, Talking Books for the Blind puts thirteen to fifteen Agatha Christies on tapes and records. And far outnumbering the visually handicapped are the four million Americans in jail. The convict librarian at a major Federal Correctional Facility in California says: 'She's the perfect escape reading. The only trouble is keeping her on the shelves. You can't trust some of these guys.'

And what about that beleaguered band that has finished school, stayed out of jail, and not yet signed up for early retirement? Do they seize on the shrinking prime of life as a respite from the endless reading and re-reading of eighty-five novels? In a sense, they do. They turn to amateur theatricals or the problems of the world. But ask a bookie for odds on the Christmas presentation of any suburban dramatic group, and he will offer you three to two that it is either *Witness for the Prosecution* or *The Mousetrap*. *The New Republic* has reconsidered Dame Agatha for serious thinkers.

Age and state of pupillage may affect how one takes Agatha Christie – neat or with a chaser – but not, apparently, personal finances. Belt tightening is now the rage and has made a mockery of Detroit's catchy little jingle: 'We like baseball, hot dogs, apple pie and Chevrolets.' Sports attendance is plummeting, hot dogs are selling at the price of steak, and automobile sales do not bear examination. Apple pie and Agatha Christie remain American favourites, durable and recession-proof. Nor is this the first time. In 1931, when banks were collapsing all over the country, *Good Housekeeping* ran its first article on Mrs Christie. In the hard years that followed, mounting unemployment, farm gluts and the flooding of the Mississippi River did not keep the *Saturday Review of Literature*, the *Saturday Evening Post* and *Time* magazine from following suit. *Time*, in fact, has paid Agatha Christie serious attention during every phase of the business cycle since, including turning points. At first glance it would appear that Dame Agatha sails serenely above the claims of prosperity or depression. But at this very moment some technician is probably correlating variations in Christie sales with fluctuations in the Dow-Jones index. And if a new economic indicator were to be born, ready to take its place with the Gross National Product and the rate of inflation, it would be a fitting memorial to the magnitude of the Agatha Christie triumph in the United States.

Measurement of a phenomenon, however, is one thing, and explanation is another. Why do Americans gulp down Agatha Christie in such quantity? Our most eminent literary critics have asked the question with genuine and growing bewilderment. Their pardonable zeal to espy a new Tolstoy or Dostoyevsky blinds them to the essence of Gutenberg's invention. They fail to recognize that, ever since the availability of the printing press, mankind has been evincing a dogged determination to read. And Americans, as usual, have taken a simple human desire and run away with it. Shakespeare and Defoe travelled west to the frontier in covered wagons. Sir Walter Scott gave birth to the mythology of the Old South. After fourteen hours a day at the spindles, mill girls in the Merrimack Valley swooned over Charles Dickens.

Now genius is just as rare in literature as it is every place else. The world has long accepted the fact that the lack of a Wren or a Bulfinch has never prevented people from erecting buildings. Instead they have settled for the nearest reliable craftsman, and left subsequent generations to discover the aesthetic excellence of the stone cottages in the Cotswolds and the wooden farmhouses of Vermont.

In the same sense, Agatha Christie has become a vernacular art form in her own right. And there is no doubt at all about the nature of her functionalism. She writes a readable book, a book that remains readable come hell or high water. This in itself is enough to explain her sales in the US, in the world.

American enthusiasts of James Joyce or Virginia Woolf do not see it this way. An embattled crew – as they have to be – they fight every inch of the way. Very well, they concede grudgingly, Agatha Christie is an honest, reliable craftsman. What's so wonderful about that? Surely there are plenty of them around. What makes this one so attractive to the American reading public?

In some circles it is tactless to reply that readable writers are not really thick on the ground. Provocative, insightful, gritty . . . yes. Readable . . . no. Narrative thrust, as we must all admit, is hopelessly old-fashioned. But then, so are most book readers, at least in this country. Coteries may be interested in the psyche; people still like stories. Agatha Christie is, *par excellence*, a story-teller.

Fortunately the second reason is less invidious. By making her works so quintessentially English, by becoming a chronicler of British small beer, Christie creates a special dimension of interest for her foreign audience, including Americans. Her intricate embroidery of

domestic trivia obscures some of her consistent defects, such as
shallow characterization and hackneyed situations. At the same time
it leaves untouched her great strengths – the absolute mastery of
puzzle, the glinting edge of humour, the accurate social eye. There
are millions of us ready to attest that this is a more than satisfactory
trade-off.

A chorus of unanimity rises on at least one of these points. Friend
and foe alike bow to the queen of the puzzle. Every Christie plot
resolution has been hailed as a masterpiece of sleight-of-hand; she
herself as a virtuoso of subterfuge. Tributes like these are heart-
warming and deserved. They are not, however, altogether accurate.
Agatha Christie's brilliance lies in her rare appreciation of the
Laocoon complexities inherent in any standard situation. She herself
rarely condescends to misdirect; she lets the cliché do it for her. When
a sexually carnivorous young woman appears on the Christie scene,
the reader, recognizing the stock figure of the home wrecker, needs
no further inducement to trip down the garden path of self-deception.
Wilfully misinterpreting every wrinkle, he will have strayed so far
into the brambles by the time of the inevitable murder that nothing
can get him back on course. Then the solution, the keystone of which
is simply the durability of the original marriage or attachment, comes
as a startling *bouleversement* for him – not to mention the carnivore.
The contrapuntal variations on this theme are explored in *Evil Under
the Sun, Murder in Retrospect* (in Britain *Five Little Pigs*), and *Death
on the Nile*.

The same deadly common sense informs the Christie approach to
impersonation and collusion. After all, any mystery aficionado worth
his salt knows how to react when a large fortune and several dubious
claimants are trailed enticingly before him. Like Pavlov's dog, he's
been there before. Then comes the grand finale, the bland Christie
assumption that, if an inheritance is worth shenanigans now, it was
worth even more one death back. Therefore – good heavens! – the
impostor is not any of those obvious suspects but is the man, or
woman, who is already enjoying full possession of the money bags.
So runs the logic of *A Murder Is Announced, There Is A Tide (Taken
at the Flood* in Britain), and *Dead Man's Folly*. The twist is then
reversed for *Funerals Are Fatal (After the Funeral)*, where the skul-
duggery begins one death later, instead of one death sooner, than
expected.

This Christie penchant for exhaustive combinations and permutations really blossoms whenever two people conspire to commit a crime. Outlandish yokings of every description abound. But, by and large, it is safe to say that whenever an obvious male ne'er-do-well exists, no woman is ineligible to be his accomplice. In this respect Dame Agatha showed her colours as early as *The Mysterious Affair at Styles*, where the gruff, middle-aged companion, complete with tweeds and walking shoes, emerges as a passionate partner in murder. From these promising beginnings she has made a clean sweep of the field, including the devoted secretary (*Sparkling Cyanide*), the protective Swedish child lover (*Ordeal by Innocence*), the subnormal housemaid (*A Pocket Full of Rye*), and the crisply independent poor relation (*The Patriotic Murders*, in Britain *One, Two, Buckle My Shoe*). Yet for a ruthless exploiter of every conceivable possibility, these achievements were not enough. The apotheosis of Christie conspiracy is reserved for *Murder in the Calais Coach*, otherwise the *Orient Express*, where everybody is guilty.

All of this lies well within the canon of the classic detective story and is deeply satisfying to those of us who like to see a rigid form explored to its outermost limits. But inevitably the further Agatha Christie wanders off the beaten track, the closer she comes to overshooting the bounds of credulity. Here is where her export market enjoys a clear-cut advantage. An English reader may boggle at palpable absurdities. Not so an American. By the time we have absorbed the larger realities of English life, together with the special aspects illustrated by St Mary Mead, we are not going to strain at gnats. For example, there is the geography of England. To American eyes, this involves an incredible number of people in a very constricted space. What's more, instead of trying to spread out, they all seem to be going to London constantly. They go there to see their solicitors, to visit their dentists, to scour the white sales. What is wrong, asks the bemused American, with the dentists of Kilchester? Is there something about the pillowcases of Wolverhampton that we do not know?

Similarly, any real estate transaction poses pitfalls for New World innocents. What exactly are these orders to view? Why is the role of the real estate so ambiguous? Who pays the rates and, God help us, are they serious about dilapidations?

The vexatious topic of class and caste naturally remains perplexing.

We Americans understand well-bred ladies in the garden and perfect gentlemen at their clubs. We are even willing to take an occasional rustic on faith. But the *terra incognita* between the two remains baffling. What do holidays camps, lipsticks from Woolworths, and family fortunes deriving from patent medicines really mean? Why are chemists, in any of their guises, automatically untrustworthy?

And there is the eternal question of age. Who counts as young, who counts as old? Above all, when do people retire? Every American, assiduously working his way through the Christie *œuvre*, can grasp the broad outlines of employment in the colonial civil services. But what is he to make of all those fifty-year-old men, coming home to marry and start families as country gentlemen of leisure? Certainly no subsequent plot-induced vagary of behaviour is going to seem bizarre after this initial monstrous aberration.

Which raises the ultimate mystification. What in the world do these people do, day in, day out? The men, including the ex-Empire-builders, are equipped with studies to which they regularly retire. For what purpose is never made clear. The ladies, lamenting the loss of pre-war domestic staffs, are all sustained by chars, foreign helps and village girls. They are certainly not pushing a vacuum cleaner around. As for children, apparently they pack their bags for school as soon as they can walk.

Even before he stumbles over a body in the library, the American reader realizes that he lacks the proper yardstick to measure normal English behaviour. What if the impersonation in *A Murder Is Announced* conjures up a hundred unexamined practical problems? It takes place in a community where no single middle-class householder seems to work for a living. Perhaps, in the ambiance of Chipping Cleghorn, practical problems automatically vanish. In *Dead Man's Folly* it might seem at first blush unnatural that an army deserter, simply by growing his beard and changing his name, could return to the home of his ancestors and escape recognition. But the neighbouring gentry are so busy snubbing the upstart that it may be safe to assume that they never take a good look at him. Then there is the marriage between Alistair Blunt and the world's greatest heiress in *The Patriotic Murders*. Why was there no press coverage to reveal its bigamous nature immediately? Here the explanation leaps to the mind trained by Agatha Christie. Alistair Blunt is a modest unassuming English gentleman who single-handedly controls the British government and world finance. If he can manage all that, he is certainly equal to the task of suppressing a few wedding pictures.

The list could continue indefinitely, but the moral is self-evident. To read Agatha Christie, an American is required to abandon all his own social experience and surrender himself to a never-never world where voices are rarely raised, where breeding is more important than money, and where a really good herbaceous border matters more than anything else. In this climate the fanciful becomes the natural, and who cares what all these people do? When we meet them, their time is fully occupied answering police questions, manufacturing false evidence, and suspecting their nearest and dearest.

If the lulling background is English, the humour is universal – at least in the vintage Christie, which can be defined roughly as running from the mid thirties through the end of the fifties. At the beginning of her career she strayed into broad set pieces, with Bundle Brent rocketing adorably around the countryside and Hastings functioning as all-purpose stooge. But with success came relaxation and the introduction of fleeting vignettes and brief asides reflecting the author's point of view. Taken as a whole, they constitute an irresistible interpretation of the human condition. Contemplate Poirot, dropping everything to fly to the assistance of a man unjustly convicted of murder. Throughout *Mrs McGinty's Dead* he discovers the object of his solicitude to be about as unappetizing a specimen of humanity as could exist this side of villainy. 'Unfortunately the more Bentley annoyed him, the more he came round to Spence's way of thinking. He found it more and more difficult to envisage Bentley's murdering anybody. James Bentley's attitude to murder would have been, Poirot felt sure, that it wouldn't be much good anyway.'

That is a very neat encapsulation of a certain kind of depressing personality and the all-too-common fate awaiting a Good Samaritan.

Then there are the two elderly women comparing appearance in *Murder With Mirrors* (*They Do It With Mirrors*). Miss Marple is undisguisedly white-haired, wrinkled and superannuated. Her American contemporary is much-dyed, much-corseted, much-dieted. But in a moment of clear-eyed vision, it is the American who ruefully admits: '"Wonderful how that old hag keeps her figure." That's what they say of me. But they know I'm an old hag all right!' Because every woman, short of the mental defectives, knows that age cannot be hidden, it can only be made more palatable.

They Came to Baghdad features a young man growing gloomier and gloomier as he describes the exalted cultural goals of his employment. In *Hickory, Dickory, Death* (or *Dock* in England) we watch a young woman conscientiously simulate an interesting neurosis in a desperate attempt to engage the attention of the young psychologist she fancies. In *So Many Steps to Death* (in Britain *Destination Unknown*) there is the splendid scene in which a would-be suicide is interrupted *in flagrante delicto* by a courteous representative of British Intelligence inquiring if she might not prefer a more sporting death. These incomparable moments are not essential to Agatha Christie's plots. They are simply her commentaries on youth, age, self-pity and courtship. Like her observations on spoiled children, village newspapers and curious neighbours, they are as meaningful in New York – and Helsinki and Tokyo – as they are in London.

For extra measure, the Christie assemblage includes a gallery of bystanders who transcend minor considerations of reality, creatures of inspired fantasy. These amiable *jeux d'esprit*, who can well be incorporated under the title of The Crazy Ladies, rarely figure as prominent members of the cast. But they are forever memorable. There is the mother in *Cat Among the Pigeons* who likes to spend her time riding around Anatolia in local buses. There is Miss Lemon, the perfect secretary, dedicated to the perfect filing system. There is Mrs Summerhayes, raising domestic incompetence to unimagined heights. And finally there are the happy interludes when the celebrated authoress takes a long cool look at the craziest lady of them all, that celebrated authoress, Mrs Ariadne Oliver.

No, Agatha Christie is not a comic writer. Black humour, mordant wit, condescending irony are – thank God – alien to her native genius. She is the author of straightforward light fiction who uses humour as leavening so that, throughout her great period, everything she wrote breathes a spirit of sanity, kindliness and detachment. It is quite enough to endear her to millions of readers.

And then, while their guard is down, she tells them more about what has happened to England since the First World War than *The Times* – either of London or New York. That quick and unerring eye for the homely detail is worth volumes of social history. In *Styles* we start out with servants, with open fires, with bedroom candles. Little by little, the servants fade away, electric lights reach the bedroom, and central heating warms good and bad alike. No one, including

The Economist, has tracked the shift of English household practice from labour-intensive to capital-intensive with such unobtrusive persistency.

Outside the home her characters, even if they are derived from a golden world that never existed, move competently through one social upheaval after another. Wartime rationing, austerity, National Health – all formed part of Agatha Christie's accurately observed England. So too did educational grants and youth hostels in London, West Indian hospital nurses and bus conductors, the very rich staying rich in a welfare state. Dame Agatha mentioned these things to us long before anybody else did because she had a noticing eye. Capital punishment disappeared for Christie malefactors, and young people left those bed-sitters with the ubiquitous gas ring in order to share apartments – and Agatha Christie registers the fact, then casually passes it on. The Empire dies, employment goes up and down, the youth movement is spawned and it is all there, as seen from the Aga stove. There is no pretension, no didacticism. But it is the record of an era, drawn dispassionately and effectively.

Even on the delicate ground of American characters, Christie rarely sets a foot wrong. Here her victory consists less in attracting a devoted American audience than in avoiding its alienation. Refined creative instinct, or a lot of horse sense, saved Christie from the fatal error of sending Hercule Poirot to New York, or Miss Marple to Washington, DC. (English readers must often yearn for a little reciprocity along these lines.) Indeed, Christie was generally sparing in her use of Americans. In her early years, she liked the hackneyed American millionaire as he appears in *The Mystery of the Blue Train* and *The Big Four*. Thereafter she began substituting home-grown products for American stereotypes. The amoral Hollywood actress in *Thirteen at Dinner* (Britain's *Lord Edgware Dies*) is English. The *nouveau riche* vulgarian in *Easy to Kill* (*Murder Is Easy*) is a local boy. Money-grubbing Babbitts are likely to hail from the City. When a touch of the wide open space is called for, she draws on the Empire, not Texas. Bronzed heroes (and some culprits) come from Kenya or Ceylon.

Naturally, when Christie's focus shifted from the manor house to the village, great wealth became less central to her plots. Still, a sinister millionaire is always useful. When she did need one, she evinced a preference for exotic Levantines, such as Monsieur Aristides in *So Many Steps to Death* and old Leonides in *Crooked House*.

We have to cross the Channel for Americans to appear in bulk. Abroad, it seems, they dominate. In *Appointment with Death* the whole cast is one large American family drifting through Jordan; necessarily the plot involves Americans interacting with each other. If nothing else, this solves the knotty problem of handling a solitary foreigner conspicuous in a multitude of English. In *Murder in Mesopotamia* the outrageous extravagance of the plot cries aloud for aliens, although nothing short of Martians would really fill the bill. And *Murder in the Calais Coach*, as all the world knows by now, was based on the Lindbergh kidnapping. The book is permeated with memories of that fateful household in New Jersey, but there are relatively few American roles and the two principal women are engaged in a masquerade throughout.

One important discovery made by Agatha Christie which seems to have eluded her competitors is that you can have the American fortune and not encumber yourself with the rough diamond who made it. In a number of her books American money has flowed into English hands, thereby producing the Lord Astor effect – namely, colossal wealth coupled to an aristocratic remoteness from its source. Linnet Ridgeway, the richest girl in England; Alistair Blunt, the embodiment of British conservative tradition; even the evacuees from London's bombing in *Ordeal by Innocence* – all are beneficiaries of some fabulous overseas Eldorado far from the current scene. In a real sense, the most consistent American character running through the works of Agatha Christie is the American dollar. And, if she had thought it out for years, she could not have hit upon a more fortunate stance, or one that accords equally well with the preconceptions of her readers on both sides of the Atlantic. That is how Europeans think of the United States, and that is how Americans expect them to think.

So much for the content of Christie's work. There is one final point to be made concerning her record in the United States. All those impressive sales figures stress the insatiable demand for her books. But there is another side to the coin. In addition to mass consumption, Agatha Christie represents mass production. Her long, hard-working life has filled the shelves with title after title. Now mystery reading often presents some of the symptoms of addiction, with the hardened fanatic devouring larger and larger dosages until a book a night is required to satisfy the craving. Everyone who has ever been bitten by the bug knows the joy of unearthing a new, appealing author, followed by the bitter discovery that his entire output consists of two volumes. With Christie, there is no such brief encounter; she is with you for life. And by the time there are over forty works to a writer's credit, re-reading becomes more than a possibility, it becomes an insurance policy. Nothing makes us feel safer than an Agatha Christie we read twenty years ago.

Not that we actually need such reassurance as long as we do not use our passports. Many harsh words have been uttered about the United States in one quarter and another, but even her most intransigent detractors have never denied the efficiency of her distribution system. Give the American middleman a mass producer on one side and a mass market on the other and he will bring the two of them together, no matter what it takes. On one level that is what this country is all about. There is no nonsense about a potential purchaser searching for a bookstore. He can find his chosen author in supermarkets, discount chains, drug stores and gas stations. If he's ready to buy, there's always somebody ready to sell. Of course there are plenty of people to deplore this kind of merchandising. Look, they whinny, at the lowering of quality, the corruption of standards implicit in such blatant hucksterism. Look at television commercials and magazines that exist solely to puff the wares of their advertisers; look at the crudity, the juvenility, the pornography littering every paperback stand. They miss the essence of a giant distribution system. It is a neutral juggernaut making no value judgements of its own. It will seed the countryside with Walter Paters as readily as with comic books. Those faultfinders who object to the crudity of the American marketplace forget that it has swept copies of Jane Austen and Henry James, as well as *Valley of the Dolls,* into places they have never been seen before. Naturally any process that deals with American magnitudes is inherently better constituted to cope with a product of multiple units than with single perfect roses. Airconditioned Cadillacs pour smoothly from the assembly line into the customers' garages. No racing driver, however, thinks he is going to get a competition machine for the Grand Prix from his local car dealer. And anybody who feels that it is a mark of worthlessness to be amenable to popularized commerce would do well to remember how much of Charles Dickens's success was due to the innovation of issuing novels in cheap instalments and the patrician disdain elicited by this practice at the time. Agatha Christie can be said to have created the perfect material for the American system of paper-back distribution. She – and her readers – could have done a lot worse.

The American Bicentennial in itself proves all this amply and graphically. In the village of Concord, Massachusetts, where it all started, there is a low stone wall bordering the approach to the rude bridge that spans the flood. This wall now bears a plaque to the memory of the British soldiers who died at its base:

> They came three thousand miles, and died,
> To keep the past upon its throne;
> Unheard, beyond the ocean tide,
> Their English mother made her moan.

Every 19 April, on the anniversary of the battle, flowers are laid on the plaque to commemorate a gallant and vanquished foe. It is fitting, it is proper and, in view of what is going on at the other end of town, it may be premature. Down the road stands the Concord Free Public Library. At last count, its card catalogue listed seventy-three separate Christie titles, without reference to multiple copies. On the same day there were two books by Agatha Christie on the shelf. The remainder were circulating. This means that all over Concord men and women were ending the day by having tea at Lyons Corner House, by taking the Underground to Paddington, by calling at the Vicarage, or by making a trunk call from the village post office. So much for the end of British influence in the colonies. Some pens, it would appear, still have victories denied to the sword.

Colin Watson
The Message of Mayhem Parva

MANY HAVE TRIED to devise some sort of apparatus of prediction in the book market. They have not had much luck. The standard recipe for the best-seller is still unformulated. It seems that one essential element remains incalculable: the equivalent to the catalyst in a chemical reaction. Agatha Christie was by no means the first writer of crime fiction to be blessed by the emergence of this catalytic function in her detective; Conan Doyle, Austin Freeman, G. K. Chesterton and A. E. W. Mason, among others, all achieved fame through a created persona; but she provides a surely unique example of how a device that has failed or achieved but moderate success in one set of circumstances may work spectacularly well in another.

Mrs Marie Belloc Lowndes, sister of Hilaire Belloc, was already fifty-two years old when Agatha Christie's novel, *The Mysterious Affair at Styles*, was published in 1920. If she read this first effort by the young wife of an English army officer, Mrs Lowndes must have been more than passingly interested in an extravagantly egotistic, moustachioed little character named Hercule Poirot, who, by virtue of long experience in the Brussels police, from which he had now retired, was able to get to the bottom of some odd goings-on at an English country house.

For Mrs Lowndes also was the creator of a self-opinionated, bossy, retired foreign detective: the redoubtable Hercules Popeau, late of the Paris Sûreté.

Stories by both authors, each featuring her own ex-policeman, were appearing in the same popular anthologies in the 1930s, so there would seem to have been no serious dispute concerning parentage. Indeed, as late as 1947, the year of Mrs Belloc Lowndes's death, there was published a Christie collection of Poirot stories under the title *The Labours of Hercules*, despite there having appeared a Popeau tale entitled *A Labour of Hercules* some eleven years previously.

The fact remains that Hercule Poirot worked whereas Hercules Popeau did not. Why? The question is one for the social historian, not the moralist. Popeau had been tailored to impress the generation that preceded the 1914 war; he was a late Victorian creation and went about things in a way the late Victorian middle class would have approved. Pushing in style, he wore 'a sardonic look on his powerful face', was thorough, not very mysterious, and given to using words like hideous, infamous, sinister – temptress even. Every inch a foreigner, certainly, but neither comical nor endearing.

АГАТА КРИСТИ

АЗБУЧНИТЕ УБИЙСТВА

(a)(B)(c)

Библиотека · Лъч ·

27

MURDO EN LA ORIENTA EKSPRESO

PARTO I

LA FAKTOJ

ĈAPITRO I

GRAVA PASAĜERO EN LA TAŬRUSA EKSPRESO

Estis preskaŭ la kvina horo en vintra mateno en Sirio. Apud la kajo en Aleppo estis la trajno pompe nomata en la fervojaj horaroj la Taŭrusa Ekspreso. Ĝi konsistis el manĝ-vagono, dorm-vagono kaj du lokaj vagonoj.

Ĉe la stupo de la dorm-vagono staris juna franca leŭtenanto, bele vestita per uniformo, parolanta al malalta viro tiom vestita, ke nenio el li estis videbla escepte de ruĝa nazpinto kaj la du pintoj de liphararo.

Estis glaciige malvarme, kaj tiu deĵoro adiaŭi gravan fremdulon ne estis enviinda, sed Leŭtenanto Dubosc bonhumore faris sian devon. Belsonaj frazoj elvenis el liaj lipoj en eleganta franca lingvo. Tamen, li tute ne sciis pri kio la afero temis. Estis onidiroj, kompreneble, kiel ĉiam estas en tiaj okazoj. . . . La humoro de la generalo—*lia* generalo—pli kaj pli malboniĝis. Tiam alvenis ĉi tiu belga fremdulo—de malproksima Anglujo, ŝajne. Sekvis semajno kurioze streĉa. Poste certaj okazintaĵoj ! Tre eminenta oficiro sin mortigis, alia eksiĝis, maltrankvilaj vizaĝoj sereniĝis, certaj armeaj ordonoj nuliĝis. La generalo—tiu de Leŭtenanto Dubosc—subite aspektis dek jarojn pli juna.

Dubosc estis aŭdinta parton de interparolado inter li kaj la fremdulo. " Vi savis nin, *mon cher*," emocie diris la generalo, " Vi savis la honoron de la franca armeo—vi fortenis la elverŝadon de sango ! Kiel mi povas danki al vi ? Veni tiel malproksimen——— "

7

Ridå för Poirot

HERCULE POIROT sitter i en rullstol när vi möter honom i "Curtain", hans sista fall. En ledsjukdom har brutit ner honom. Hans gamle vän kapten Hastings beskriver honom som en liten hopsjunken man med skrynkligt ansikte. Det är pa-

---

AGATHA CHRISTIE: Curtain. 2.95 pund. Collins.

---

tetiskt uppenbart att den korpsvarta hårfärgen kommer från en flaska.

Det är på Styles Hastings och Poirot möts. Herrgården är numera ett gästhem. Bland de betalande gästerna finns en mördare.

På Styles började Poirot sin bana för drygt 55 år sedan. I "The Mysterious Affair at Styles" ("En dos stryknin") träffades han och Hastings för första gången.

Inte ens 1920 var den belgiske detektiven med de stora choserna och de små grå cellerna någon ungdom. I "Curtain" bör han vara uppemot 140, så han har rätt att verka lite sliten.

Men det är bara Poirots yttre som är präglat av ålderdomens obarmhärtiga angrepp. Hjärnan fungerar. Också denna sista gång överlistar Poirot alla, inklusive kapten Hastings. Det sker dock på ett sådant sätt att han kostar på sig ett litet, tämligen rumphugget moraliskt resonemang i slutkapitlet.

Att kapten Hastings låter sig luras är inte så konstigt. Han har kallats deckarlitteraturens största åsna. Precis som i Agatha Christies tidiga Poirotdeckare fungerar han som "the idiot friend", ett slags resonansbotten för problemlösarens geniala utläggningar. Modellen är givetvis Sherlock Holmes vän dr Watson.

Det sista Agatha Christie gjorde, innan hon dog, var att ta livet av sin gamle detektiv Poirot, som tjänat henne troget i 55 år

I "Curtain" är kapten Hastings dotter med. Det komplicerar allt; hon kan ju vara mördaren – eller ett tilltänkt offer.

"The Mysterious Affair at Styles" har betecknats som den bästa deckare en debutant någonsin skrivit. Det är möjligt, men till Agatha Christies bästa hör boken inte.

Det gör inte heller "Curtain", som skrevs för drygt 30 år sedan och i ett bankfack fått vänta på en för Poirots död lämplig tidpunkt. Men "Curtain" är kvalitativt överlägsen det mesta som numera produceras i who-done-it?-genren.

Det är en sentimental resa Agatha Christie tar oss med på. Man gör gärna färden; den är ju deckarhistorisk.

Med ett rörande brev tar Poirot avsked av kapten Hastings och av miljoner läsare. Han erinrar om gångna "jaktdagar".

– They were good days, säger han.

Visst har han rätt.

JAN MÅRTENSSON

Murder International. *Above left :* The jacket for the 1968 Russian edition of *The A.B.C. Murders. Above right :* A review from the Swedish *Sydsrenska Dagladet* ; just two of the 103 languages into which Agatha Christie's books have been translated ; and to whet Esperanto-readers' appetite the first page of *Murder on the Orient Express (left).*

Poirot, though also a foreigner, was decidedly an eccentric, a bit of a joker. He was short and his head was noticeably egg-shaped. His eyes had the curious quality of turning green when he was excited. He was an incorrigible moustache-twirler. He carried a cane, smoked queer little cigarettes, was a fancy dresser and dyed his hair. He spoke English with laughable literalness ('I beg that you do not disarrange yourself, monsieur') and was always making quaint remarks about the power of thought. A Froggie, for a cert.

But of course Poirot was not a Froggie. He was a Belgian. And the distinction was more important in 1920 than it might seem today. Military propaganda had created an image of 'gallant little Belgium' that persisted long after the war. Within such a picture, Poirot's five-feet-four stature, his limp, his bold moustaches, fitted perfectly. Even his fastidiousness was tolerable, whereas it would have been considered odious affectation in a Frenchman, one of those unpredictable ex-allies who were throwing their weight about in Europe just when England wanted only to put a wreath of Earl Haig's nice poppies on the beautiful new Unknown Soldier's Tomb at Westminster and then settle down to crosswords and detective stories. For such diversions were playing no small part in the attempt by the middle classes to get their nerve back and ignore the irrational and disconcerting things that other people, in other lands, continued so wantonly to do.

The truth is that Poirot was neither French nor Belgian. He was as English a creation as one of the new 'Moorish' picture palaces, or boarding-house curry, or comic yodellers. Personifying native conceptions of continentals, he was immediately familiar to readers and therefore acceptable. As a detective, he was dedicated to the righting of wrong (the trade of our national saint, no less) and to the defence of property and social order. The public was used to these vital matters being entrusted to stern, authoritative, slow but fairly realistic operators on the Inspector French model; now dawning, though, was the age of novelties, and an unconventional investigator made a nice change. Especially attractive was the man's apparent omniscience. Every encyclopaedia salesman knows that the English stand in awe of knowledge but resent intelligence. Poirot was skilfully modelled to seem mysteriously, fascinatingly knowing, yet with a monumental cockiness that restored him to favour as 'a bit of a card'. How could anyone fail to smile at such amiable absurdities as: 'Ah, it was a clever plan, but he did not reckon on the cleverness of Hercule Poirot!' or 'But I am a good detective. I suspect. There is nobody and nothing that I do not suspect.'

In the years when Mrs Christie's reputation was being built, there was no way in Britain of tapping massive readership overnight. In the absence of television and before the organization of the film 'promotion' industry, authors had little help along the road to fame other than an occasional press interview and, very rarely, a patronizing and carefully non-committal airing on the wireless. Books, even cheap editions, were between hard covers, and they were sold in bookshops or from the railway bookstalls of the W. H. Smith monopoly, which could, and did, soft-pedal the offering of any book of which it happened to disapprove on moral or political grounds. There was still no sign of the paperback tide that eventually would sweep into grocery stores and sweet shops, hotel foyers and airport lounges. The novelist's main hope was to receive the custom of libraries, and of these the most useful to the writer of entertainment such as detective stories was the private lending or 'chain' library that flourished in every suburban and provincial high street. The records of one such library in a West Country town were quoted at the time as showing the issue of 6,000 books every week to its customers in a population of 43,000.

Nothing quite like the 'chain' library exists on that scale today, but during the inter-war years it was virtually the only source of reading matter for those who could neither afford to buy books outright nor find the kind of undemanding entertainment they wanted in the public libraries, with their emphasis on non-fiction and 'serious' novels.

Having discovered in 1932 that in Britain 'book buying has not increased in proportion to literacy', Mrs Q. D. Leavis observed 'that the proportion of fiction to non-fiction borrowed is overwhelmingly great, that women rather than men change the books (that is, determine the family reading), and that many subscribers call daily to change their novels'. The authors she quoted as being typical purveyors to the 'tuppenny dram-shops', as she called the chain libraries, included Sax Rohmer, Edgar Wallace, William Le Queux, E. Phillips Oppenheim and 'Sapper'. Perhaps she selected these on account of their special reprehensibility and decided to let Agatha Christie off with a private caution, for by that time the detective story, as distinct from the thriller, shocker, or 'blood', was beginning to be accorded a sort of self-conscious patronage by the intellectuals, much as the juvenile japery of P. G. Wodehouse was to become a literary 'in thing' a generation later. Nevertheless, even by the early 1930s the request for 'another Christie' was to be heard daily at the counters of the chain libraries, where seven Poirot novels were already in stock and two featuring Miss Jane Marple, the refined but shrewd resident confidante of the village of St Mary Mead.

What was there in these books that pleased the predominantly middle-class but by no means exclusively middle-aged people who read and praised and recommended them to one another? Firstly, it must be said that they provided what the average library customer understood by 'a good read'. They were written in a sound, simple, undemanding style and were free of literary affection of the kind that had bedevilled the work of so many of the early mystery writers. Their plots, though ingenious, were not convoluted to a tiresome degree, nor did they depend upon the technical or esoteric. Avoided were all subjects offensive or controversial, but there ran unobtrusively through their pages a simplistic commentary upon human nature that somehow left the reader with the flattering impression that he had been given credit for philosophical astuteness. Thus Poirot: 'Life is like a train, Mademoiselle. It goes on.' Gosh, how true, the reader would echo.

To describe books designed for entertainment – detective stories, thrillers, Westerns, romances even – as 'escapist' may be convenient but it is not always accurate in context. Consider a typical small but flourishing suburban lending library of the late 1920s, in Lower Addiscombe Road, East Croydon. It was a clean, newly decorated, well-lit shop, as quiet in atmosphere as the monastic-styled public library in nearby Ashburton Park, but with a much more raw, exciting smell: instead of leather and waxed wood, here were thick, pulpy paper and new ink and shiny yellow covers whose pungent scent seemed redolent of the scenes so dramatically depicted upon them and featuring, singly or in combination, corpses skewered with oriental daggers, delicate ladies in straight-cut frocks suppressing gasps of horror with three fingers (reversed), and men rendered incognito by excessively slouchy hats and grasping guns like great slabs of liquorice. Many of these covers bore identifying ciphers. A scarlet circle proclaimed Edgar Wallace, the words *for Excitement* in dashing black script followed the name of Sydney Horler, like some confident medical prescription.

Such a library opened daily and remained open until late in the evening. Husbands home from the city might then accompany the wives who, at other times, would regard 'changing the books' as part of the shopping and go in for a new Zane Grey or Ethel M. Dell between buying a few mixed pastries from Clark's cake shop and choosing cheese and bacon from Sainsbury's, before whose glacial-tiled walls a man in white stood all day deftly sculpting half-pounds of butter with a pair of wooden paddles. Just as his seemed a full-time job, so was that of the librarian who stamped the stream of outgoing books and took the tuppences and threepences on all those Oppen-heims and Glynns and Jefferson Farjeons and Wallaces and Agatha Christies.

By definition, 'escapist' literature all.

But what those respectable, placid and, in general, reasonably secure citizens of Addiscombe might have wished to escape *from* is not immediately evident. Not, certainly, from the hardship and squalor that afflicted great numbers of people in the industrial areas. Nor from the deep and abiding poverty of the agricultural labourers. Compared with them, the clerks and civil servants and shopkeepers and salesmen who were forming the colonies of commuters around London and other big cities had already arrived at a desirable existence.

Escape from dullness, then? From the monotony of the daily circuit, the triviality of suburban social intercourse, the narrowing of physical and spiritual prospects once the first few payments on the mortgage had been made? That is a more persuasive supposition, particularly in relation to the popularity of 'high society' novels with their portraiture, so often splendidly spurious, of gracious living at the top; also of the Ruritanian fantasies of Anthony Hope and Farjeon, and of P. C. Wren's sand-strewn exoticisms. However, the detective story – specifically as conceived by Agatha Christie – cannot qualify as escapist in any such obvious sense.

It offered more subtle comfort.

Addiscombe and its hundreds of counterparts elsewhere may have seemed safe and peaceful, settled and pleasant, but the world outside was manifestly none of these things. The Great War had only recently relinquished the last of the fathers, brothers and sons lucky enough to survive and bring back their souvenir shell cases and Jerry bayonets for the embellishment of an English fireplace. Europe was in a mess. Russia had gone Bolshie. Even at home, where the economy had settled into slow subsidence, troops had been called out against strikers and unemployed and the unthinkable had briefly come about in the shape of a police strike. Small wonder that Mrs Belloc Lowndes's brother, Hilaire, pronounced England 'done' – though the actual immediate cause of his despair was not industrial strife but the mechanization of farming.

The middle class, the Addiscombians, might have been largely insulated from these worrying matters by distance and a press dedicated to the Northcliffe canon 'Give the public what it wants' to a degree not far short of asininity, but hints of present trouble and intimations of dark future possibilities did filter through. It was not very nice to see – as one did every day then – the limbless ex-soldiers begging in the gutters and the bands of locked-out miners who had walked from Wales to sing for pennies outside Wilson's coffee shop or the Zeeta restaurant. Here was inescapable evidence that something was amiss, and only the most complacent or obtuse could dismiss it with that attitude of censorious contempt shown by detective novelist Dorothy L. Sayers to those she called 'out-of-works'.

Agatha Christie, in her written work at least, seems to have been virtually apolitical. The emphasis throughout her books is upon the value of common sense in solving crime, which we see as a flaw in a canvas of ordinariness. True, a printed verse about the unemployed which crops up in *Sing a Song of Sixpence* as a clue to the desperate nature of a suspect (he proves to be the murderer) is described as 'trashy', but that could as easily be a literary comment as a political one: poetry other than the 'proper' kind received short shrift in England between the wars. And although, in 'The Kidnapped Prime Minister', references to the advocacy of international negotiation and to pacifism with a capital letter are unmistakably disapproving, Mrs Christie takes care not to make them herself but to put them into the mouth of the monumentally thick Captain Hastings. It is Hastings also who is made to say, as if making casual mention of a self-evident fact, 'now that war and the problems of war are things of the past . . .' And that was about as much political argument as the buyers and borrowers of books really wanted to hear in those days.

Poirot himself personified an orderly and sensible approach to such

Overleaf: A case of mistaken identity, perhaps,
as Agatha Christie comes face to face
with her wax portrait in the Grand Hall
at Madame Tussaud's.

problems as refused to be things of the past but kept irrupting into the present, despite the efforts of politicians. British politicians in the 1920s were invariably elderly men in frock coats and top hats who kept up a rapid, convivial strut in front of newsreel cameras, at which they nodded a great deal; they liked to be called statesmen, not politicians. Poirot, too, might be a strutter, but he had an appealing continental politeness, was whimsically aware that to be foreign is to be funny, respected True Love, British Justice and Le Bon Dieu, and, albeit rarely, was capable of acknowledging his own human

frailty ('I, Poirot, am the imbecile! Hurry, Hastings, and let us hope we are not too late!') It mattered little that a great deal of his apparently deeply significant reasoning eventually proved to have almost nothing to do with the case. Readers felt that here was true intuition – the sort of thing all too obviously lacking in the top-hatted gentlemen on the newsreels.

If the little Belgian habitually postponed giving society the full benefit of his power of deduction until the last or penultimate chapter, by which time the law was three or four corpses down, no reader was

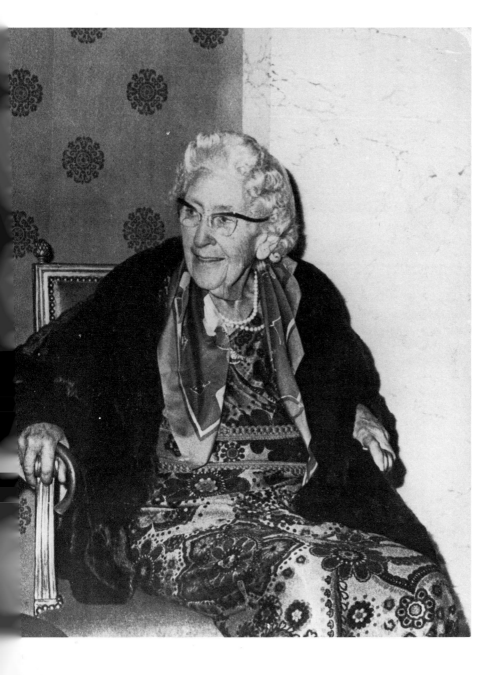

ungracious enough to observe that on a points system it was always the murderer who won. The stories, after all, had been written not as academic exercises in logic but as diversionary entertainment. For the customers of the Oppenheim and Le Queux type of thriller writers, there had been provided transport into a land of riches and romance, of beautiful women and handsome men, where millionaires and maitres d'hôtel abounded but where no one, apparently, ever delivered milk or drove a tram or went home to Oldham or Ongar. Agatha Christie and her imitators offered something very different. It was a dream, but not of marble halls. The vision was one of familiar homeliness and it was populated not with gamblers and duellists and international jewel thieves, but with stock characters from village and suburb who observed rules of behaviour according to station, and were isolated utterly from all such anxieties and unpleasantness as were not responsive to religion, medicine, or the law. In book after book they appeared: the diffident, decent young pipe-smokers; plucky girls with nice complexions; the assorted house-party guests, for ever dressing for dinner or hunting missing daggers; the wooden policemen, crotchety spinsters, gruff colonels, woolly-minded vicars; and the ubiquitous chauffeurs, butlers, housemaids and the rest of the lower orders, all comic, surly or sinister, but none quite human, their talk modelled on middle-class notions of the vernacular of shop assistants and garage hands.

The setting for the crime stories by the Christie, or Mayhem Parva, school was generally a hybrid between village and commuters' dormitory somewhere in the Home Counties, self-contained and substantially self-sufficient. There would be a church, well attended by regulars, and an inn with reasonable accommodation for visiting detective inspectors. There might be a library and a village institute as well as the police station, and the several shops might include a chemist's where weed killer and hair dye would conveniently be stocked. In the larger, set-apart, houses would dwell a doctor, that irascible colonel, a successful businessman, perhaps an eccentric or, much the same thing, an artist, and a moneyed old woman given to bullying her dowdy companion and mucking about with her will.

There would exist for these people none of the sordid and intractable problems of the real world, such as growing old or losing faith or being abandoned or going mad. Even that favourite plot device, the incurable disease, would be introduced smoothly and painlessly.

Of course, one of the characters would have to get murdered – perhaps two or three or more – but death was almost invariably off stage. For the regular Christie reader the fact of murder soon acquired a sort of bland inconsequentiality, like getting into the Honours List.

England as represented by Mayhem Parva was as much a mythical kingdom as any realm of musical comedy, but the fantasy derived from nostalgia, not invention. It was a fly-in-amber land, in which were perpetuated the ways and the values of a society that had begun to fade away from the moment of the shots at Sarajevo. 'Stands the Church clock at ten to three? And is there honey still for tea?' Rupert Brooke had asked, and, ignoring their favourite, because dead in the war, young poet's sardonic undertones, the English middle-class townies desperately wanted the answer to be yes because Grant-chester (wherever that was) sounded just the place to have a bungalow when father took his pension: an old-fashioned, picturesque sort of place, where there would be a nice church service if you wanted to go, and the doctor's surgery wouldn't be crowded, and the grocer would deliver.

The word 'cosy' has often been applied to the work of Mrs Christie and her followers, and in no contemptuous sense. Their choice of setting is believed by many to have been calculated on the principle that the eruption of violence in the midst of the familiar, the respectable, the ordinary, is more shocking – hence more satisfactory as a device of fiction – than the presentation of evil in a locality itself unusual or sinister. The theory is attractive, and it is true that a few writers have succeeded in creating a sort of cottage Grand Guignol. Very occasionally, Agatha Christie herself seems to be trying out a chill, but she is ready at the first sniff of scepticism to disown the idea and return to that good-natured, slightly spinsterish urbanity with which she normally treats of crime in Mayhem Parva. After all, it would require a singularly confident, self-regarding writer to suppose her readers to be really horror-stricken by the discovery of a corpse in the tea tent at the church garden fête. Standing aghast is an indulgence to be kept to a minimum in the detective story, the policy of whose writers in the 1920s and 1930s was to make the griefs of the characters short and formal and to hurry everybody along to the interviews in the library in good time to dress for dinner – a social obligation that not even the most extravagant multiple of homicide could be allowed to disrupt.

Those English families who were changing their library books as regularly as they changed the accumulators in their battery-powered wireless sets had no desire to be harrowed or depressed by either medium. The immeasurable carnage of the recent war was a curiously private obscenity, brooded over by the tired, quiet men who had come back. Only now were those who had remained at home beginning to learn that whatever they thought they had shared with the men overseas in those four years, it was not the war. And out of the silence of the returned soldiers and the fear of the others lest they hear the unendurable, there was formed a vacuum in which, for more than twenty years, little but the trivial and the fatuous and the make-believe seemed capable of flourishing. And games. Games were the thing to cheer everybody up. In those two decades began the process whereby game-playing became first a preoccupation, then an obsession, and ultimately, when re-named sport, a national religion.

The detective-story game was a puzzle, pure if not simple. It was related to real life only in respect of a common vocabulary and a set of mores epitomized by Poirot's declaration: 'I have a bourgeois attitude to murder. I disapprove of it.' This game did not require belief in the commission of a crime in the sense of finding room in the mind for the true blackness of spilled blood, for its haunting smell, for the pitiable surprise upon a murdered face. One noted instead the game's familiar counters, harmless as play money: gun, dagger, paperweight (what an unconscionable number of paperweights people seemed to need in Mayhem Parva), poisoned thorn, spreading stain, tumbler smelling of almonds, watch-glass smashed at 5.24, expression of terror as if . . ., acrid reek of cordite. Did the victim matter? No, not really. Sympathy for the departed was never solicited, even by implication. He or she was generally someone widely disliked: someone rich or with expectations of wealth; someone powerful, malevolent or mean; very often an extortionist; sometimes a character hiding former criminality behind a presently prestigious appearance. An innocent or venerable person scarcely ever got murdered. Just as rare was the death of a pretty girl, although one subject to moral lapses would seem to have been expendable. The rule against the slaughter of children was absolute.

To deplore the two-dimensional nature of these stories is to miss the point of why they were written in that form. They could not have offered what they did – relaxation and, in a subtle way, reassurance –

The Queen meets the First Lady of Crime at the première of
the 1974 film production of *Murder on the Orient Express*.

if they had possessed that third dimension which gives a book the power to affect the reader in much the same way as actual experience. Mayhem Parva was a flat representation of a community blessed with contentedness and regulated by what people who do not much care for explorative thought call 'common sense'. It featured neither dramatic heights nor chasms of desperation, just the neat little hedges of the maze, the puzzle, at whose centre awaited a mysterious figure labelled Murderer. This figure inspired no dread, merely curiosity.

One cumulative effect of constantly reading this kind of fiction might have been to blunt temporarily the fear of death. The circumstances of the murder were seldom credible enough to be really shocking. On the other hand, the victim's death was so often described as 'instantaneous' that it must have encouraged in the reader the personal hope that lingering ends were exceptional. Finally, the inevitable solving of the puzzle, the identification and rendering harmless of the murderer at the end of the game, somehow had the effect of cancelling out the death or deaths that had gone before. It made the world seem a safer place. And that, in any age, is one of the most devoutly desired of delusions.

Celia Fremlin

The Christie Everybody Knew

DETECTIVES incredibly stupid
  And villains unspeakably vile,
The usual presence of Cupid,
  The usual absence of style.
A heroine brave and resourceful,
  Dread poisons, infernal machines,
A hero alert and of course full,
  Whenever they down him, of beans.

THUS (with three further stanzas of similar import) does a *Punch* reviewer of 1925 dismiss his current batch of detective stories, including, it so happened, one by Agatha Christie. There was little sign at this period that *Punch* (usually an incomparable seismograph of current sociological trends) had as yet recognized the name 'Agatha Christie' as being anything at all special. True, her second book *The Secret Adversary* had been favourably reviewed some three years earlier, but this seems to have been a single swallow, heralding nothing. Since that review was to be almost the sole attention she was to receive from *Punch* for many a long year, it is perhaps worth quoting. 'The cleverest thing about this most fresh and attractive mystery is that Miss A. Christie has succeeded in keeping her adversary secret up to the very end of the book. It rankles, honestly, to have to confess to such fallibility, but the fact is that I made up my mind time after time as to which unlikely character was the evil "Mr Brown", the "Man behind Bolshevism", only to decide, after I had read a few more pages, that I had been wrong in my guess.' When the now-famous name was mentioned after this, comments tended to be brief and patronizing for many a year. Thus of her collection of short stories, *Poirot Investigates*, the critic remarked: 'The more I read of detective fiction, the sorrier do I become for the assistants of these wonderful unravellers of crime. Unblushingly, Miss Christie allows Poirot to pour contempt on Captain Hastings, and I found myself hoping with all my might that Hastings would turn and rend the great man.'

After this little stir of recognition, silence descended (as far as *Punch* was concerned) for a decade or more. A few lukewarm lines were devoted to *The Blue Train* (1928), and to *Murder at the Vicarage* (1930), and that was all. It was not that *Punch* simply disdained detection-writers as being beneath their notice. On the contrary, writers such as Mrs Belloc Lowndes, Francis Grierson, John Rhode and others were given generous space in the 'Booking Office' columns.

However, there were journals of the period that were beginning to recognize the name of Agatha Christie as something new and important. The *Daily Express* in particular seems (to its great credit) to have spotted her in the very earliest days of her career; and though I have been unable to trace in their columns any actual review of her first book, a subsequent reviewer of *Murder on the Links* wrote: 'No one who read *The Mysterious Affair at Styles* will need reminding of the fact that Agatha Christie stands in a class by herself as a writer of detective stories.'

Alone among the contemporary newspapers, the *Express* seems to have recognized Agatha Christie as 'news', even as early as 1922. In January of that year, they are already treating her as enough of a VIP as to rate a twelve-inch interview, complete with photograph – a plump, schoolgirlish face under a schoolgirlish velour hat. 'Crime is like drugs,' said Mrs Christie in this interview. 'Once a writer of detective stories and, though you may stray into the by-paths of poetry or psychology, you inevitably return – the public expect it of you.'

'The public expect it of you.' Already, then, at the beginning of 1922, Agatha Christie had a public, a band of devoted and importunate followers, though as yet beneath the notice of *The Times* and the *Daily Telegraph*.

Who were this public? At this distance of time, of course, the echoes are faint. Those of the early fans who survive are well into their sixties or beyond. From this age-group I sought memories of the first impact of Agatha Christie. A retired British Rail manager, aged seventy-four said: 'I can't remember which one I read first, but I do remember that I couldn't put it down, and after I'd finished it I couldn't rest until I'd read the lot. I'd get up at five to read them before I started for work. I'll never forget those summer mornings.' And a housewife, aged sixty-five, added: 'She was already a famous name, I suppose, when I first came across her – about fifteen or sixteen I suppose I was. I remember having a vague feeling that my mother disapproved of her.' An aeronautical engineer, aged sixty, also had memories of a certain illicitness: 'I read *The Seven Dials Mystery* all through in church, hidden under my prayer-book!'

In 1926 there came, of course, the Great Divide in Agatha Christie's career: the year of her disappearance, and also of that most controversial – and, in the opinion of many of her admirers, the best and most powerful – of her books, *The Murder of Roger Ackroyd*. The clamour aroused by the identity of the murderer has even now not entirely died down. In serious studies of the detective novel it is still debated as hotly and as inconclusively as it was at the time of publication. Opinions of critics then ranged from 'a brilliant psychological *tour-de-force*' to 'a rotten, unfair trick' – and they still do. 'The best thriller ever!' chortled the *Daily Sketch*, while 'tasteless and unforgivable let-down by a writer we had grown to admire' growled the *News Chronicle*.

The heat generated was extraordinary, and there are people alive today who still, after half a century, are ready to boil all over again at the memory of that long-ago shock-ending. A great-grandmother, aged eighty-two said to me: 'I couldn't believe it! I just couldn't! That our very own Agatha Christie should do such a thing to us! It spoilt her books for me ever afterwards.' And a doctor still practising, aged seventy-six, exclaimed: 'I thought it was awful . . . so unfair! And making him a doctor, too! I'd just qualified, and I felt it was an insult aimed at me personally, at the whole medical profession. That a doctor could be a murderer . . . I thought it was wicked. I still do . . .'

Whatever may have been its merits or demerits, there is no doubt that *Roger Ackroyd*, and the storm surrounding its publication, put Agatha Christie firmly and for ever on the map. From now on, her name rapidly became a household word, as did that of her detective, Hercule Poirot; indeed, it was not long before he was by way of becoming a national figure of fun. 'Above all, there is Hercule Poirot, with his egg-shaped head,' remarked a *Daily Express* reviewer. 'The suggestion of the shape of the head is a stroke of something like genius. It is so vague that it haunts. Was the egg right-way up, or upside-down, or sideways? There is no clue to the solution of this mystery.'

Within the next decade, Hercule Poirot and his egg-shaped head had become part of our cultural heritage, and writing send-ups of him was more or less a national sport. With great good humour, Agatha Christie herself occasionally joined in the game, as (for example) in an interview she gave to the *Daily Mail* in 1938: 'Let me confess it – there has been at times a coolness between us. There are moments when I have felt: "Why – why – why did I ever invent this detestable, bombastic, tiresome little creature? . . . eternally straightening things, eternally boasting, eternally twirling his moustache and tilting his egg-shaped head . . ." Anyway, what *is* an egg-shaped head . . . ? I am beholden to him financially . . . On the other hand, he owes his very existence to me. In moments of irritation, I point out that by a few strokes of the pen (or taps on the typewriter) I could destroy him utterly. He replies, grandiloquently: "Impossible to get rid of Poirot like that! He is much too clever."'

And he was too. His career was now unstoppable, his place in our national culture unassailable. By the end of the thirties, he had featured in an important murder trial, that of Horace Budd, accused of poisoning a certain Francis Cyril Newlands. In summing up, the judge remarked (on the alleged method of poisoning) that: 'Even in the most dramatic stories in the realm of detective fiction, there has surely never been a similar instance. I do not think that M. Poirot or any other great detective of fiction has ever had to deal with such a case.'

But despite the growing fame of Poirot and his creator throughout the thirties, and despite their millions of fans, the review space given to Agatha Christie in most papers remained niggardly, and the reviews for the most part less than ecstatic. 'Pleasantly readable' was the kind of phrase used; 'a clever twist' and 'a writer of remarkable virtuosity'; and often there was a sting in the tail of even the most favourable notice such as the *Sunday Express* notice of *Murder on the Orient Express*: 'This provides one of the most remarkable and improbable solutions ever offered by a detective story writer, but Mrs Christie writes with such unfailing humour and high-spirits that its improbability does not bother the reader in the least.'

Even the wholly laudatory reviews of this period tend to be slightly arch in tone, as if the reviewer is anxious to assure his readers that he does not really set much store by this sort of thing. Thus a *Daily Telegraph* reviewer in 1930: 'How many vicars must long to murder their church wardens, and here is one who actually has the luck to find one murdered in his study.'

Unsympathetic reviews continued numerous during this decade, forming a substantial minority of all press comments. Critics delighted to pick holes in the plausibility of the Christie plots, and to fasten on points of detail. 'Who in their senses would use hammer and nails and varnish in the middle of the night within a few feet of an open door?' asked *The Times*, reviewing *Dumb Witness* in 1937. 'And do ladies wear large brooches in their dressing-gowns?'

Sometimes, the critics were not merely hostile, but downright unfair, and when this happened there was invariably an outcry from Christie fans. On one occasion, no less a personage than John Dickson Carr (then Secretary of the Detection Club) took up the cudgels on her behalf. The occasion was the appearance, in the *Evening Standard* in 1938, of a review by Howard Spring of *Hercule Poirot's Christmas*. Mr Dickson Carr protested: 'Mr Spring has carefully removed every element of mystery. He discloses (a) the identity of the murderer, (b) the murderer's motive, (c) nearly every trick by which the murder was committed, and (d) how the detective knew it. After this massacre it is safe to say that little more harm to the book could possibly have been done.'

But in the teeth of reviews unfair, mediocre, patronizing, or downright hostile, the popularity of Agatha Christie's books rose like an unstoppable tide. In the autumn of 1935, the *Daily Express* ran *The A.B.C. Murders* as a serial, setting up simultaneously a column of 'Readers' Guesses' to the solution. But a Mr R. A. Harman of West Norwood, while congratulating the paper, also carped: 'How can M. Poirot hope to solve an ABC murder when he cannot read this publication to his best advantage? He is anxious to reach Churston, and so takes the midnight train from Paddington, arriving at 7.15. Had he looked more carefully, he would have found that by leaving nearly two hours later – 1.40 a.m. – he would have arrived an hour earlier – at 6.10 a.m.' It was Mrs A. V. Freshfield, of Wanstead, who got the solution 'Correct in every detail' and wrote: 'I suddenly felt I knew the murderer, the motive, alibi, everything . . . I decided to write it down, and send you the result herewith.'

With virulent detractors, passionately devoted fans, and ever-creasing press coverage, Agatha Christie by the end of the thirties was already becoming one of the famous names of the world. Her books were reported to be the teenage Princess Elizabeth's favourite reading. 'Queen of Crime' was by now her acknowledged title. It had already been said of her (and has been quoted hundreds of times since) that she 'made more money by crime than any woman since Lucrezia Borgia'.

Perhaps most flattering of all, she had become a butt for humorists who felt no need even to mention her name, so sure were they of the public's recognition. 'But in whose Library was the body originally found?' enquires a puzzled cartoon policeman in *The Humorist* of 1938 when confronted by a motor-accident. And in *Reveille*, a forensic scientist is depicted peering down a microscope and asking testily for the 'little grey cells'.

Then came the war. At the outset, many were the literary prophets of doom, total eclipse being widely predicted not only for Agatha Christie, but for the whole genre of detective fiction. Who, demanded columnists far and wide, was going to be bothered with fictional death and horror when the real thing was going on all around them? Millions, apparently. To the astonishment of sociologists, critics – and even of writers and publishers – the reading of detective stories not only showed no decline but even, during the winter of the Blitz, showed an unmistakable increase.

In his book *Murder for Pleasure* Howard Haycraft reported that, in the London shelters during the Blitz, 'raid' libraries were set up which, in response to popular demand, lent out detective stories and almost nothing else. This rather startling finding was amply corroborated by a Mass Observation survey of reading which reported: 'Of detective authors mentioned, Agatha Christie certainly tops the poll at the moment.' A fifty-year-old widow confessed in an interview: 'I always used to look at the end first, but I don't now. Now I like to have to concentrate. The suspects, and working it all out – you know – it soothes your nerves.' 'Many people', the report continued, 'would appear to have a special feeling for Agatha Christie, over and above their general preference for detection and mystery. "Cosy" and "comforting" were words used over and over again.'

The feeling of comfort persisted after the war. A teacher at a Polytechnic, now in her forties, recalled to me what the books had meant to her in a lonely and miserable period of her youth when she faced for the first time the realities of bed-sitter life in London. 'Agatha Christie was my one comfort and support during those first desperate weeks. I had never been away from home before, and I was lonely and depressed beyond anything I can describe. The one thing that made it endurable, going back to that awful little dark room in the evenings, was knowing that my Agatha Christies were waiting for me there. I had all of them, mostly in paperback, a whole shelf of them, I caught sight of them as soon as I opened the door, it was like coming home. People say that the Agatha Christie characters are cardboard, but if they are, then cardboard friends were what I needed at that time. I felt so close to them . . . so secure in their company.'

That very same autumn it so happened that Moscow also was

devoting some attention to the Agatha Christie books. 'A deliberate attempt by the Cripps–Bevin–Attlee–Churchill hyenas . . . to distract the attention of the masses from the machinations of the war-mongers,' was the Soviet verdict. Nor was this the last time that Agatha Christie was to incur the disapprobation of a Communist régime. After her death, Hong Kong's leading Communist paper, *Ta Kung Pao*, described her as a 'running dog for the rich and power-ful' and accused her of having 'described crimes committed by the middle and lower classes of British Society without ever exposing their social causes'.

Despite such reproofs, Agatha Christie's books continued to go from strength to strength. In 1948, the publication by Penguin of ten of her best-known stories marked a new high in her career. A first printing of 100,000 of each of these books was followed, over the next two years, by further reprints, totalling over two million copies in all. As remarked in the *Observer*: 'Between now and the end of the year, some four or five million members of the island race will have been seduced, captivated, misled, mystified, titillated, surprised, startled, and altogether thoroughly entertained by the acknowledged queen of crime-fiction the world over.'

For the following two decades and more, praise was so sustained as to become almost tedious to quote. As Julian Symons asked in his review of *Cat Among the Pigeons* in the *Sunday Times*, 'What fresh words can one find to praise Agatha Christie, that infinitely cunning and various serpent of Old Nile?' Lacking fresh ones, reviewers for the next decade and a half had to make do with the old words and phrases. 'Brilliant', 'incredibly ingenious', 'incomparable skill' and so on fill the columns devoted to her work. Only here and there does one encounter a dissident voice, such as that of Francis Iles in the *Sunday Times* reviewing *Hickory, Dickory, Dock*, a mystery set in a multi-racial students' hostel: 'It reads like a tired effort. The usual sparkle is missing, the plot is far-fetched and the humour too easy (all foreigners are funny, but coloured foreigners are funnier).' But on the same Sunday Maurice Richardson was saying in the *Observer*: 'One is pleased, though not in the least surprised, to find her so vociferously sound on the colour problem.'

There is just one of her books during this halcyon period over which a shadow fell, albeit one utterly outside the author's control and in no way reflecting on the quality of the book in itself. The book I refer to is *The Pale Horse*, published in 1961; and at the time of publication it received every bit as much praise as its predecessors – 'brilliantly ingenious' (Violet Grant, in the *Daily Telegraph*) was typical of reviewers' opinions. It was eleven years later that the book encountered a brief but harsh spell of criticism when the horrifying case of Graham Young, the mass-poisoner, was filling the headlines. It was noted by many people at the time – both journalists and ordinary citizens – that this real-life poisoner had followed a method terrifyingly similar to that of the fictional criminal. The *Daily Mail* set out in meticulous detail the resemblances between the two cases and quoted 'a senior detective' as saying of the fictional hero, 'This is Young to a T.' Agatha Christie was reported as being 'naturally upset' by this unnerving resemblance between the recent atrocity and the plot of a book she had written more than ten years before – though the fact that Young's bookshelves were 'crammed with poison reference books' may have reassured her; she could hardly have taught him anything he did not know already.

So we come to the final phase – a sad one, indeed, for those of us who have enjoyed Agatha Christie's books for as long as we can remember. In *Curtain*, published in 1975, Poirot – to a sigh of dismay all over the world – actually died. But he triumphed in death with newspapers on both sides of the Atlantic printing mock obituaries, a unique tribute to a fictional detective and to his creator.

Dorothy B. Hughes
The Christie Nobody Knew

EVERYONE KNEW the Agatha Christie who created Hercule Poirot. She was the clever Christie, the one who thought up all manner of intricacies to tempt the attention of the reader and of the little Belgian detective. Almost as many knew the Mrs Christie who wrote of Miss Marple, illuminator of the English village, a lady in the complete sense of the word, genteel and imperturbable. In later years she would become a part of the Christie self-portrait. There were many who knew the Christie who, more or less as a pastime, wrote of that bright young couple, Tuppence and Tommy. And certainly, known to all her admirers was the Christie of centre stage, she who proved a writer could be at one and the same time equally successful as a playwright and as a novelist.

There was yet another Christie whom nobody knew, or so few as to amount to almost nobody. This was Mary Westmacott. Even today, and even in book circles, there are more who do not know than who do know her true identity.

Agatha Christie became Mary Westmacott in 1930 to write an unmystery novel, *Giant's Bread*. It caused rather less than a sensation. Four years later, Mary Westmacott tried again. Her second novel, *Unfinished Portrait*, like the first, made little to no imprint on the literary annals of the season.

And so, Mary Westmacott disappeared. For ten years. Until 1944, when once again she entered the lists. It would seem her return was because she had a story that had to be told, a story which Agatha Christie could not tell. It was *Absent in the Spring*, and it is *la crème* of her small body of works. As before, all the beauty and emotion she poured into a work was as a libation wasted upon barren earth. She followed this one in 1947 with *The Rose and the Yew Tree*. It created no more stir than its predecessors.

Five years elapsed before she tried again. In 1952, *A Daughter's a Daughter* appeared, and in 1956 *The Burden*. They were received with the same lack of interest. With these she completed her six-novel offering. This was the end of Mary Westmacott's career.

Why? Why the waste of six unusual books, six fine books, six books which encompass some of the best of Christie's writing? There is no reason why anyone should pay a lick of attention to my answer to my question. True, it comes from a good many years of observation of the way of books. But it is no more than a personal opinion.

In my opinion then, Mary Westmacott's work was mishandled.

Why else, before the secret was out, when it was no more than a murmur, was there always the addition of that disparaging throwaway line, 'not very good, woman-type stuff'. Woman-type indeed! As if Christie under whatever name would fashion a damozel shrinking through cold stony hallways and winding towers, her heart given to a dark and dour character whose bad manners and worse temper she mistakes for dislike, not affection, until the final passionate Gothic embrace. Or that Christie would have wasted her time telling of some silly modern girl who takes herself up into attics and down into cellars when she knows there is a killer loose and that she holds the clues to his or her identity.

The Westmacotts bear as little relation to women-type novels as to Winnie-the-Pooh. One cannot but wonder if any of those who proffered opinions had ever read her work. Had they, they would know that in its own way, each of these books, whose heroes lead lives of quiet desperation and whose villains are villainous only in that they do not understand, presents a fragment of the human comedy. Each tells a tale of the procession of days which add up to the years, and which resolve not in a crashing dissonance but in a whimper. And life goes on, but down a different lane and to a different bird call.

These are works in which Christie is trying to fathom herself and those who were a part of her world. The stories are the revelations of a woman of perception, a woman who is searching human emotions to preserve and heighten moments which must be remembered. She is writing of men and women whose dreams bleed when pricked, who are not beset by the gods or the fates, but who are made bereft by human frailties and a wanton expenditure of the loving heart.

Not by any catch-phrases can Westmacott be put into a Christie category. The books are not concerned with 'breathless romance, intrigue and suspense . . . tangled lives and star-crossed passions . . . dangerous secrets', as has been written of them. Westmacott was a distinctly different person from the mystery writer, Agatha Christie.

The six books are actually all a part of the same book. In the whole they are the fictionalized autobiography of Dame Agatha. Properly the autobiography begins with the second, *Unfinished Portrait* (1934). Christie could not have given many interviews before that time, at least not about her childhood and youth, or the Mary Westmacott identity would have been revealed immediately. In *Unfinished Portrait*, Larraby, a portrait painter, frames the story, thus making the pretence that it is a story, not a personal revelation. Yet there can be no doubt that Celia, the unknown woman he presumedly met and spoke with, is Christie, so much younger than others of her family that she is in effect an only child, the beloved of her mother.

Mary Westmacott writes beautifully of children: 'Then there were the things you thought about in the daytime. Nobody knew that as Celia walked sedately along the road she was in reality mounted upon a white palfrey. (Her ideas of a palfrey were rather dim. She imagined a super horse of the dimensions of an elephant.) When she walked along the narrow brick wall of the cucumber frames she was going along a precipice with a bottomless chasm at one side. She was on different occasions a duchess, a princess, a goose girl and a beggar maid. All this made life very interesting to Celia, and so she was what is called 'a good child', meaning she kept very quiet, was happy playing by herself, and did not importune her elders to amuse her . . . Celia seldom asked questions. Most of her world was inside her head. The outside world did not excite her curiosity.'

The book tells of her father's illness and early death, her mother travelling in grief, while the child lives with her superb grandmother:

In figure she was majestically stout with a pronounced bosom and stately hips. She wore dresses of velvet or brocade, ample as to skirts, and well pulled in round the waist. 'I always had a beautiful figure, my dear,' she used to tell Celia. 'Fanny – that was my sister – had the prettiest face of the family, but she'd no figure – no figure at all! . . . As thin as two boards nailed together. No man looked at her for long when *I* was about. It's figure the men care for, not face.' 'The men' bulked largely in Grannie's conversation. She had been brought up in the days when men were considered to be the hub of the universe. Women merely existed to minister to these magnificent beings.

The character of Grannie in part prefigures Miss Marple.

Grannie was never idle. She wrote letters – long letters in a spiky spidery handwriting, mostly on half sheets of paper, because it used them up, and she couldn't bear waste. ('Waste not, want not, Celia.') Then she crocheted shawls – pretty shawls in purples and blues and mauves. They were usually for the servants' relations. Then she knitted with great balls of soft fleecy wool. That was usually for somebody's baby. And there was netting – a delicate foam of netting round a little circle of damask. At tea time all the cakes and biscuits reposed on those foamy doilies . . .

And again:

The night air, Grannie said, was highly injurious. Air of all kinds, indeed, she regarded as something of a risk. Except on the hottest days of summer she rarely went into the garden, such outings as she made were usually to the Army and Navy Stores – a four-wheeler to the station, train to Victoria, and another four-wheeler to the stores. On such occasions she was well wrapped up in her 'mantle' and further protected by a feather boa wound tightly many times round her neck.

It is this grandmother who takes the little girl on train trips to London, where they lunch at the Army and Navy Stores, and Celia is introduced to the magic of the theatre. All of Christie's girlhood is herein, the musical year in Paris, the fashionable season in Cairo, the suitors and the proposals, the love marriage which became the failed marriage, and which broke her beautiful world apart. In the end is the repetition of the beginning, as she, the mother, is raising an only daughter. There is even included in this story her own explanation of her strange disappearance and of an amnesia which was less forgetting than dreaming. *Unfinished Portrait* is told with a minimum of plot, in its stead is remembrance of times past. The portrait is unfinished as her life was yet unfinished.

The first Westmacott, *Giant's Bread* (1930), was autobiographical only in bits and pieces. It would seem to be the story of others she knew, knew closely, composites to be sure because few if any writers go in for the verities in their portraitures. Little Vernon has the same good no-nonsense nurse that Celia will have, he even has the identical nursery wallpaper with 'mauve irises twining upward'. Both children have dear imaginary playmates before meeting with real children. Both are dreamers, of course, for the child Vernon, when not fictional, is the child Celia.

What was the word – the magic word? Brumagem – that was it – Brumagem. An enchanting word! The Princess Brumagem! A word to be repeated over to himself softly and secretly at night . . . Sitting on the slippery chintz, he frowned perplexedly. He had a sudden imperfect glimpse of two Mummies. One, the princess, the beautiful Mummy that he dreamed about, who was mixed up for him with sunsets and magic and killing dragons – and the other, the one who laughed and said, 'Aren't children too *funny*?' Only of course they were the same . . . He fidgeted and sighed.

'What's the matter, Master Vernon?'

'Nothing,' said Vernon. You must always say, 'Nothing.' You could never tell. Because if you did, no one ever knew what you meant . . .

Vernon, a girl cousin who comes to live with him and his mother, and a small London boy on the next estate, are inseparably tangled in each other's lives in maturity as well as in childhood.

In *Giant's Bread*, there is what must be mentioned, to us of the post-Hitlerian period, a familiar form of anti-Semitism. Yet Mary Westmacott, the product of her culture, her class, and her times, might well have considered her handling of Sebastian to be one of forthright liberalism. Vernon is an anti-hero, years before they became fashionable. Sebastian is the stable and sympathetic character, a Cambridge graduate, eventually an important London impresario, who is an intelligent businessman as well as a man of impeccable artistic taste. Westmacott's attitude to him must be little different from Queen Victoria's to Disraeli. He was a beloved friend, a man of fine character, brilliant in all respects, but always, the Jew.

In the ten-year period when Mary Westmacott lay fallow, Agatha Christie was, as we know, a whirlwind of activity, moving from honours and triumphs to the topmost Alp of the mystery field. Here she would remain. Yet Mary Westmacott could not be forgotten. She had more to say, and it could not be said in the medium in which Agatha Christie worked. The mystery novel, like the theatrical play or the sonnet, is contained within a prescribed pattern. The writer may wander a bit but not far, not and stay within the form.

When Mary Westmacott returned in 1944, she brought with her *Absent in the Spring*. Shakespeare gives the title and introduces the theme of the story, 'From you have I been absent in the Spring . . .' Of all the books created by either Christie or Westmacott, this one, even if it was born to blush almost unseen, must have given the most complete satisfaction, possibly even the exaltation which comes so rarely to a writer. For this is the perfect story, simple, bittersweet, ironic, expressing the heartbreak of love unfulfilled yet fulfilled.

The story concerns Joan, a wife and mother, who has never questioned her own values, who has managed a charming home for her husband and her three children, who has always done the proper thing. That her children married young to get away from home; that her husband, who wanted to farm the land, not become a solicitor, has retreated into himself, are facts which would never occur to her. Until she is marooned at a desert way-station *en route* from Baghdad, where she has been visiting her younger daughter, to Istanbul. She finishes reading her two books. She quickly uses up her bit of writing paper. And she is left with nothing, nothing but to learn about herself. Through her, Westmacott says that unless you have heights and depths, you are missing life, that there is a richness in the lives of those who know suffering, and an 'arid nothingness' in those who keep themselves insulated. In her blinding moments of self-revelation, Joan becomes aware of the love her husband had for another woman in their village, a woman who, to her, was nothing, nobody.

Little wonder the exquisite quality of this book was not discovered, when one reads that it concerns 'a husband's secret life' and 'the mysterious hold that beautiful Leslie Sherston had for him'. Compare Westmacott's design for Leslie Sherston: 'She walked through disillusionment and poverty and illness like a man walks through bogs and over plough and across rivers, cheerfully and impatiently, to get to wherever he is going . . .' The gallantry of Leslie and Rodney makes 'the unbearable bearable' as Archibald MacLeish said of poetry.

The theme of the desert, which is noted in one way or another in all the Westmacott books, is fully developed here. Westmacott distils the great clarity of desert light, the space and infinite solitude which compel a person to look into himself. And which also compel a person to know the presence of God. Perhaps the Westmacott readers alone are aware of what a strongly religious person Mrs Christie was. Prayer was a way of her life and the presence of God an integral part of living.

It is only meet that her next book should be inspired by both poetry and religion. The introduction and title of *The Rose and the Yew Tree* are from *Little Gidding*, the final section of T. S. Eliot's *Four Quartets*. 'The moment of the rose and the moment of the yew tree are of equal duration.'

The story is a retelling of the legend of Beauty and the Beast. But Westmacott does not accept its progress as simply a fairy tale. She asks: Why? What impels Beauty to go by choice with the Beast? Why does she offer herself as sacrifice for him? The answer to all is love. Love which can be completed only in sacrifice. Yet this answer does not probe deeply enough for the author. Metaphysically she advances to the question: 'Does one ever really have a choice about anything?'

We do not know if Mary Westmacott became possessed by the riddle of time through her preoccupation with Eliot's poetry. Or if it was her dwelling upon the riddle which led her to Eliot. We do know that the theme of time is interwoven through all of the books, in the later ones in some depth. She ponders it in *The Rose and the Yew Tree*, but she does not evolve her final answer until *The Burden*, where, in the character of Mr Baldock, she states: 'The truth is, we're all slavishly obsessed by Time. Chronological sequence has no significance whatever. If you consider Eternity you can jump about in Time as you please. But no one does consider Eternity.'

It is no less in its people than in its themes that the books are all of a piece. Characters move from one setting to another, putting on a new name or face. Mr Baldock is part the nurse and part the grandmother, crusty but kind of heart. He is described as having a chair at the university, with a small cottage in the village where Laura, leading character of *The Burden*, when a little girl of ten, becomes his friend. On his first appearance he has invited Laura to tea but pretends he has forgotten the invitation. Later he tells her that he only made this pretence to see what she would say, and to have her see him as he is, 'a rude, ungracious old curmudgeon'. The tea he serves her is a child's dream tea, 'currant buns, jam roll, éclairs, cucumber sandwiches, chocolate biscuits and a large indigestible-looking rich black plum cake'. Laura gives 'a sudden little giggle', and confirms: 'You did expect me. Unless – do you have a tea like this every day?' 'God forbid,' said Mr Baldock. In another passage, his character is revealed in his reaction to a glimpse into Laura's dream world. '"Bad butter," said Mr Baldock. It was one of his expressions of perturbation. "Bad butter! Bad butter!"'

Mr Baldock is the only rock of Laura's world, both when she is a child and as an adult. As Nurse is Vernon's security, and, during her mother's illness, the grandmother is Celia's. Dame Laura in *A Daughter's a Daughter* may be a noted Harley Street practitioner, but in her more sophisticated habit she is the same commonsensical wise woman as Nurse and Nannie and Grandmother.

She is also in part another of the self-portraits of the later Christie: '"Like all old women, even if I am a distinguished one, I preach." She drains her glass of buttermilk and asks, "Do you know why I drink this?" "Because it's healthy?" "Bah! I like it. Always have since I went for holidays to a farm in the country. The other reason is so as to be different. One poses. We all pose. Have to. I do it more than most. But thank God, I know I'm doing it."'

It is through these character actors that Westmacott comes to terms with life. They are Chorus, wise, understanding, pragmatic.

The final two books, although entirely separate in the story sense, are at one in their theme. Sacrificial love destroys, not redeems. Oddly enough Westmacott uses the same name for a lead character in both. In the first, Dame Laura is the strength which manages, just, to save the mother and daughter from each other's devotion. In *The Burden*, Laura is the sister who takes on the burden of love. This is not the only instance where Westmacott repeats herself. Jim Grant, the freckle-faced boy farmer of *Unfinished Portrait*, becomes in *A Daughter's a Daughter* Jim Grant, army officer. One would consider it mere carelessness save that the books could not have been written carelessly, they are too finely wrought for that. It is true enough that most authors cannot remember character names from the opening to the closing of a book. Nevertheless with a favourite Christie character, which Dame Laura is, it is difficult to believe that in the very next book the name would be used again for a prominent character, not without purpose. Perhaps these oddities compose a cryptogram which we shall decipher when the yet unpublished Christie papers give us the proper clues.

For all the pain of living, these are not unhappy stories. There is in them affirmation of life, not its negation. Furthermore they give added values, such as we learned to expect from Christie in her sunset years. And there are moments of fun.

One of these extras comes in the closing book with Mary Westmacott's little lesson to readers. It may be a put-on, but it is more than that. Particularly for those who never learned to read Mary Westmacott properly. Mr Baldock asks the child Laura: 'How do you read a book? Begin at the beginning and go right through?'

When she replies, 'Don't you?' he tells her: 'No, I take a look at the start, get some idea of what it's all about, then go on to the end and see what the fellow has got to say and what he's been trying to prove. *Then* I go back and see how he's got there and what's made him land up where he did. Much more interesting.'

Laura says: 'I don't think that's the way the author meant his book to be read . . . I think you should read the book the way the author meant.' And the irrepressible Mr Baldock declaims: 'The reader's got rights too. The author writes the book the way he likes. Has it all his own way. Messes up the punctuation and fools around with the scene any way he pleases. And the reader reads the book the way *he* wants to read it, and the author can't stop him.'

J.C.Trewin

A Midas Gift to the Theatre

I

IT IS WELL OVER fifty years since 'the world's greatest thriller' – so its management said – John Willard's *The Cat and the Canary*, reached London to the jingle of a distich:

> If you like this play, please tell your friends;
> But pray don't tell them how it ends.

To give away a puzzle is a darker crime than anything done on stage. That was why so many were furious when an evening-paper critic of *Towards Zero*, out of tune with Agatha Christie, revealed the murderer's name in his last paragraph, indeed the last three words. A rare lapse; no one has repeated it. (In any event, the piece survived for six months.) Through the years playgoers and critics joined in keeping any secret Mrs Christie confided to them, and her trust was honoured; it astonishes us now that after a quarter of a century in London *The Mousetrap* can still be acted before audiences with no idea of its development or climax.

Agatha Christie, by herself, wrote twelve full-scale plays (one published, not performed) and three in a single act. She collaborated in another full-length play; four more, from her novels or short stories, were adapted by other hands. It was fitting, I think, that her final one-acter, *The Patient* (1962), depended on its curtain-line. Whatever else was wrong, nobody sustained a problem as she did, or solved it so quickly without a tedious explanatory huddle. This was her Midas gift to the theatre. 'Upon my soul,' exclaimed Dickens's Barnacle Junior, 'you mustn't come into the place saying you want to know, you know.' Agatha Christie's fans did want to know. In the later plays they may have found it a lagging wait. Never mind: having been in at the death they insisted on a post-mortem verdict.

By the time she had fully arrived, a dramatist on her own, what someone christened the Deep Freeze period had ended. These were plays, often American, in which a writer used unscrupulously any kind of effect that might chill. It might also be comic; he had to risk that. *The Cat and the Canary* began about midnight (ideal for a will-reading) in an isolated house by the Hudson River, twenty years to the hour after the testator's death. The place, with adjustable panelling, was staffed by a West Indian Negress and a farcical house-maid – possibly in curl-papers; I am not sure. Characters included a Keeper of the Asylum. About the same season the cast of another play, an English one planked down surprisingly in deep Norfolk, contained a Modern Girl (the dramatist's capital letters), a Secret Service agent, an American Orientalist, an Indian butler, a Chinese servant, a handy man, and Kali, a Manchurian leopardess. Thrillers then could have grabbed a classic epigraph: 'Nothing is but what is not.' Everybody was either someone else or an irrelevant eccentric. John Gielgud, as a young actor, fought through a rattle-trap entitled *The Skull* (a detective as its criminal): it was established in a deserted church with a ghostly organist, and, as Gielgud said resignedly, a comic spinster in difficulties, an old professor with a cloak, and a cockney sexton with a club-foot, to help the thing along.

This was not Agatha Christie's way. Her characters could be waxwork, but there was never a leopardess in sight. Agreed, in *Spider's Web* she did admit a sliding panel. 'It would be very convenient for holding a dead body, wouldn't it?' said a schoolgirl, Pippa Hailsham-Brown (in the brisk voice of Margaret Barton); and certainly it was: one of the few concessions, quietly tongue-in-cheek, to a method that had faded while Agatha Christie was first writing. At its meridian, but not at hers, we could have counted upon a stage bitumen-black or steeped in a sickly green, a flapping of bats in the belfry, complex work with trap-doors, and quite likely a blackmailer sending to his victim 'quintets of cocoa-beans to call up memories of old days in Africa'.

2

Agatha Christie seems to have been in the theatre for generations. Yet she had only one produced play of her own – *Black Coffee*, no cocoa-beans – until the coming of *Ten Little Niggers* in 1943. She thought so little of her first piece, efficient and scarcely remembered now, that she dated it in an article as 'about 1927: I believe it came on for a short run in London, but I didn't see it because I was abroad in Mesopotamia'. A kindly word to her past; a lost drift of pollen. It was years before Ivor Brown would say of her, as Britain's most popular dramatist: 'Agatha Christie is incapable of seeing two or three living persons gathered together without imagining a third who has ceased to live. Lounge-hall immediately becomes mortuary.'

I was brought up to the drama in a town in south-west England. A fair touring date, there was also a small and vigorous Repertory.

So we were able, at a long remove from London, to observe its fashions and contortions, its panelwork, scrawny hands and misty phosphorescence; multiple disguises and mad scientists in cellars; seldom a leopardess because these were awkward to travel, but plays called invitingly *The Gorilla* and *The Monster*; after these a sequence of corpses in the library. The later puzzles were predictable. They gave us a spurious sense of power. Either it was so obviously the parlourmaid that it couldn't be, and therefore was; or else X was an actor of so much standing that his last-act flourish was obligatory.

About this time Agatha Christie, who would never be predictable, appeared with *Black Coffee*, produced in 1930 at Swiss Cottage, and in 1931 at the St Martin's (where *The Mousetrap*, brought from next door, would settle forty years on). Francis L. Sullivan as the Belgian Poirot, handling the Amory murder case, had Roland Culver as his Watson, Captain Hastings. Soon the play turned up at our Repertory in its precise and applauded sorting and docketing of clues. If the Poirot here was unrecognizable, that was hardly alarming; the stock-company actor had already supplied Hanaud in *At the Villa Rose* with the same fluff of mannerism and the same accent, standard fittings for a European detective.

Black Coffee was not Poirot's stage début; the effervescent fellow had arrived at the Prince of Wales Theatre (1928) in *Alibi*. Discreetly but firmly adapted by the veteran Michael Morton from *The Murder of Roger Ackroyd*, its solution startled any newcomer. I suppose most older London playgoers recall it for the presence of Charles Laughton. During his first few London seasons this young man, plump and protean, would come on as a Hungarian tramp, a Czarist general, a glossy American millionaire, Agatha Christie's detective ('entirely unlike him, but a wonderful actor,' she said generously), a half-paralysed Dublin footballer, a slightly sinister Mr Pickwick, a red-haired sadist, a farcical brigadier, and an oleaginous gangster – 'oily' is too simple. It could have been half the cast of a Deep Freeze play.

Laughton and Christie did not meet again on stage. During the 1930s she continued to let other dramatists speak for her in the theatre though we gather that she would have preferred the work herself. She did write, but left unprinted, a play so far from routine that she was probably diffident about it. The year was 1937, date of her novel, *Death on the Nile*, which was dramatized a decade later. A visit to Luxor, where she saw Howard Carter, had inspired the elaborate

Poirot's stage début was in *Alibi* (an adaptation of *The Murder of Roger Ackroyd*) in 1928, when he was 'admirably impersonated by Mr Charles Laughton', in the words of *The Sketch*.
Above : Poirot (on the right) surveys the body of Ackroyd (Norman V. Norman, centre), with Dr Sheppard (J. H. Roberts).
Below : A classic Christie denouement as Poirot convicts each witness of lying.
Opposite : The Graphic was impressed with Laughton too, and paid a full-page pictorial tribute to his performance.

POIROT CONVICTS EACH WITNESS OF LYING : L. TO R., DR. SHEPPARD (J. H. ROBERTS), MAJOR BLUNT (BASIL LODER), FLORA (JANE WELSH), POIROT (CHARLES LAUGHTON), MARGOT (CONSTANCE ANDERSON), RALPH (CYRIL NASH), URSULA (IRIS NOEL), MRS. ACKROYD (LADY TREE), PARKER (HENRY DANIELL), AND GEOFFREY (HENRY FORBES ROBERTSON).

EXPRESSIONS OF A SLEUTH

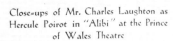

Mr. Charles Laughton, the twenty-six-year-old actor as he is in real life

"Monsieur l'Inspecteur, il est bête comme ——" Poirot is amused at the clumsy methods of the local police

"Englishmen conceal only one thing—their love." The detective in one of his philosophical moods as a rest from sleuthing

"I appeal to you, Mees Flora—tell me ze truth." The relentless Poirot in plaintive mood

"Each one of you has something to hide." Poirot grows suspicious of everybody

Poirot at work. The effective curtain to Act I, when the detective sits alone in front of the murdered man, turns down the lights, and mentally reconstructs the crime

"Poirot may play the fool, but there is a reason behind his actions," he says to the unsuspecting criminal

"To me it grows clearer." Poirot has a clue which he keeps to himself

"Ze person who killed Sir Ackroyd is in zis room." The detective in one of his "je sais tout" moods

frieze of *Akhnaton*, not published until 1973 and as yet unperformed; it might have suited the crowded portrait-gallery of the 1930s, everyone welcome from Socrates to Jane Shore, Parnell, and Victoria Regina. In three acts, ten scenes, and an epilogue, a span of more than sixteen years, with nine changes of set and a cast of twenty-two, supers aside, she yielded to an indulgence that has affected other dramatists. History suddenly grasps them. Thus Ben Travers, high master of English farce, wrote – he hoped anonymously – a searching portrait of Saint Paul, *Chastity My Brother*. It was undervalued because news of his authorship filtered out: a writer had to stay in his own 'field'. Eden Phillpotts left behind him an unperformed drama, *A Comedy Royal*, from 1067 in the city of Byzantium.

Agatha Christie went back 2,500 years beyond this in a dignified, bloodless pictorial tragedy, with ceremonial prose that never achieved eloquence. It dramatized the fate of King Akhnaton, his wife Nefertiti, and his attempt to supplant the old religion of Egypt and to overthrow the priesthood. Akhnaton himself ran a high temperature, but the people in general were as remote from us emotionally as they were in time. Mrs Christie was eager to enliven them. A stage direction read: 'Down L. Akhnaton is putting the final touches of colour to the well-known sculptured head of Nefertiti.' In the less sombre moments Nefertiti's sister, Nezzemut, could talk like this: 'Being Queen of Egypt is quite wasted on you. I'd have done it so much better. The King is so dreamy and moody – he needs someone to wake him up – to – to *run* him!'

The play remained, presumably, on Agatha Christie's desk. In the theatre other dramatists had taken over. Frank Vosper, self-confident, often witty actor who was lost at sea, based *Love From a Stranger* (1936) on a Christie short story, 'Philomel Cottage', expanding it into an able Fat Boy drama ('I wants to make your flesh creep'). He cast himself as the homicidal colonial wooer of the girl who, dangerously, had won a sweepstake. After a loitering start, the third act had visitors to the New Theatre fainting from anxiety, a throw-back to Grand Guignol. Next, the *Ghost Train* driver, Arnold Ridley, restored Poirot (Francis L. Sullivan once more) in a version of *Peril at End House*. Sound enough; but by then it was the spring of 1940 and real life had dimmed the Theatre Theatrical.

After these, with a couple of exceptions, Agatha Christie would walk alone. In *Ten Little Niggers* (1943, St James's; directed by Ivor

Brown's wife, Irene Hentschel), she disposed, one by one, of most of the guests and servants – we had a general, a judge, a doctor, a spinster, and so forth – isolated on Nigger Island off the South Devon coast. A wholesale murder puzzle, contrived with perfect sangfroid, its success dismayed the experts. C. B. Cochran, who ought to have known, told Mrs Christie that, though he would have done it, his backers (clearly without historical sense) thought it impossible to have so many people dying on the stage: 'It would just make audiences roar with laughter.' It did not; and in time it proved to be one of the only two Christies to carry New York. There (421 performances) it was re-titled, tactfully, *Ten Little Indians*.

With its disembodied voice, progressive ornament-smashing, and strengthening tension, this was one of those plays that are magnetic in performance, though in a day or two we cannot quote a line. The rest of Agatha Christie's acted work followed it within nineteen years. The only other thriller-dramatist who wrote so resolutely was Edgar Wallace, and he packed his plays into a far briefer space. Reckless and impatient, he asked for large companies and expensive sets; tempted by Deep Freeze methods, he was not above organ-music and a hooded figure in a vault. Except in *Witness for the Prosecution*, which was privileged, Agatha Christie did keep her casts in hand; a management's model dramatist, she was invariably thoughtful. Peter Saunders, the impresario who staged eleven of her plays, counting the triple bill, records that a first script of *The Mousetrap* – two sets and a cast of ten – was rather too much for his resources at the Ambassadors Theatre. Next day Mrs Christie returned with the script rewritten and one of the sets and two actors deleted.

Apart from certain scenes on the Nile, in Jerusalem, and in Petra, which derived from Middle East journeys with her archaeologist-husband, Agatha Christie kept as a rule to country houses where a plot could turn round. Hence the drawing-room at Copplestone Court in Kent, with priest's hole; the Great Hall of Monkswell Manor in Berkshire; Sir Claud Amory's house at Abbot's Cleeve; the Garden Room at Sir Henry Angkatell's; and sundry mansions in South Wales, near the Bristol Channel; Devon, and homicide-ridden Cornwall. A generic title would have been *Murder at a House Party*. She had an ear for titles. Oddly, 'Murder', which her audience needed, figured in only three. During her last years, when she was a guest at a writers' conference, another guest told his neighbour – a

local dignitary's wife – that he had acted in *Murder in the Cathedral*.
She nodded: 'Ah, yes, that would have been one of Agatha's.' (Not
everyone knows that Eliot's title was the inspiration of Henzie
Raeburn, actress-wife of the director, Martin Browne).

3

Agatha Christie put action before character. Too often, in early plays
or late, her people were stereotyped. Like Wilde's minor epigrams,
they could have been transferred, as needed, from plot to plot, hall
to manor, court to vicarage: a doctor there, a spinster here. Attendants
on a body, they rarely had life of their own. Naturally, we remember
Poirot – even he could be something of a stereotype – and Mrs
Boynton in *Appointment with Death*, Romaine in *Witness for the
Prosecution*, Clarissa in *Spider's Web*, and Lady Angkatell in *The
Hollow* do linger. Others can coil out in a greyish procession of names.
Who were Lady Melksham, Justin Fogg, Bryan Wingfield, Inspector
Japp, Miss ffolliott-ffoulkes, Kay Strange, Michael Starkwedder, and
Mr Mayhew? Uncertainty, I daresay, is ingratitude. Even if they
might as well have answered to numbers, they did everything required
of them; collectively, a disciplined shoal of red herrings. No addict has
time or wish to complain during a performance; but after the event
a Christie programme can be unhelpful. Who (if I may ask teasily)
were Giles Ralston and Amyas Crale?

The contrast between the characters and the things they did was
soon visible. Few of the people in *Appointment with Death* (1945)
kept any appointment with life. I recall the play for its Middle
Eastern décor; for a cave in a rose-red cliff at Petra where the matri-
archal Mrs Boynton, created by Mary Clare, sat like an unpleasant
idol as she drowsed and later died. Poisonous and poisoned, she had
been a hypnotist and a wardress in an American gaol. Others round
her were so dimly traced that we could hardly bother about them.
Frank Vosper, with his actor's awareness, had seen his characters
more acutely in *Love from a Stranger*. Led by Ivor Novello (as the
homicidal maniac), Diana Wynyard, and Margaret Rutherford, this
was the first play sent, with a portable theatre, to the Normandy
invasion front.

It was 1951 before Agatha Christie moved permanently into the
West End scene. During the previous six years she had had only two
plays, one her own, one an adaptation. Her *Murder on the Nile* (1946),

in spite of its background and a grand actress, Vivienne Bennett, never got going. True, an authoritative clergyman (synopsis speaking) would 'lay bare an audacious conspiracy' in the saloon of a Nile paddle steamer. Someone was shot in the knee; someone else was shot while lying in a bunk. Finally, it was apparent that a romance between 'a more than usually eligible young man and a downtrodden girl would soon ripen into matrimony'. Good; but I wish today that the bells rang louder. *Murder at the Vicarage* (1949), at the Playhouse – once, tautologically, the Playhouse Theatre – was Moie Charles and Barbara Toy's treatment of the novel. Resuscitated in 1975, it trailed into a second year, longer than the original run, on the talismanic strength of Agatha Christie's name above the title: enough to pull in audiences and to blast the critics. The piece was a skein of cross-questions and crooked answers in the vicarage study, as busy as a market-place while the vicar, his wife, his nephew, his curate, his maid, his neighbours, all from stock, prowled round to confuse us in the matter of Colonel Protheroe's murder: a problem teased out by the most ardent gardener and knitter in St Mary Mead.

Eighteen months after the *Vicarage*, Agatha Christie ruled her own stage. She would be helped again only once (in *Towards Zero*); and she was about to begin the central period on which, in the theatre, her fame depends. The summer of 1951 brought *The Hollow*, her first play under Peter Saunders's sage management; in its early months it would restore the Fortune Theatre, a little house opposite the Drury Lane colonnade that had reminded Sean O'Casey of Falstaff's page looking across to his master. The theatre's name had often seemed ironic; but now puzzle-plays were scarce and audiences took gratefully to this one (from the Christie novel) about the death of an unloved doctor, a week-end guest at a house in the Home Counties.

Misguidedly perhaps, Agatha Christie delayed his murder until the beginning of the second act, though she held her solution as usual until the ebb of the third. Practically everyone wished to kill the man; *The Hollow* was like an armoury bristling with weapons. Earnestly we hoped that he would be shot; and once he was, the evening itself shot along cheerfully, Jeanne de Casalis, radio's 'Mrs Feather', presiding as a vague creature called Lady Angkatell whose left and right hands were inevitably at odds. The dialogue was lively. The detective came credibly from Scotland Yard. Under Hubert

Gregg, later a prolific Christie director, the piece ran at the Fortune, and later the Ambassadors, for 376 performances. A good score, it would soon look meagre. On 25 November 1952 Peter Saunders, who had leased the Ambassadors in West Street behind Charing Cross Road, a compact drawing-room house renowned for its wartime revues, put on a new thriller, *The Mousetrap*.

4

We need another word for this kind of play. 'Whodunnit' is clumsy, 'thriller' merely a mild label. 'Thrill' has lost the potency of its Elizabethan usage when Juliet cried, 'A faint cold fear thrills through my veins,' and Claudio trembled at 'the thrilling region of thick-ribbed ice'. Theatrically the word must be an everlasting umbrella for everything between the grinding mechanical alarums of *The Bat* (from the primeval Deep Freeze) and such a closely-manoeuvred puzzle as *The Mousetrap*. With this title, proposed by her son-in-law, Mrs Christie added a laugh to contemporary Shakespeare. At *Hamlet*, III.ii.232 (for let us be exact) the king asks tetchily after the wordier part of the play scene: 'Have you heard the argument? Is there no offence in't?'

HAMLET: No, no, they do but jest, poison in jest. No offence i'th' world.
KING: What do you call the play?
HAMLET: The Mouse-trap . . .

In any *Hamlet* revival now the company holds its breath. Someone will laugh responsively and irrelevantly. An audience is whisked out of Elsinore and 'the image of a murder done in Vienna' to the Great Hall of Monkswell Manor. (Mrs Christie might have found the earlier *Mousetrap* a trifle obvious.) Her title was a second choice. To begin, and in the grimmest of all nursery snatches, it had been *Three Blind Mice*, the name of the story she adapted. (That itself had originally been a radio sketch.)

Theatre historians will revel in asking why *The Mousetrap*, never to be compared with that 'knavish piece of work' at the Danish court, grew as it did into the world's longest runner. We have no dramatic reply. People kept on going to the Ambassadors. Peter Saunders nursed the play at a time, not far into its third year, when most managers would have withdrawn it. Clearly it owed a lot to 'word of mouth', the theatre's imponderable asset; news of Monkswell Manor must have spread between the Shetlands and Scilly.

In the West End's uncertain mosaic it keeps steadfast. A second generation acknowledged it as a form of Stonehenge. Legends expanded: the tale of a couple who returned annually to the theatre of their engagement night and saw *The Mousetrap* twenty times. (By now they have had a change: the play is next door at the St Martin's.) With all this we may forget that here is a really efficient thriller of its time. A disproportionate run – well, yes. And for many people who have almost forgotten it, or who have never been, the subject is a safe and easy joke. It is a highly valuable one. Today, at the core of the West End, is an untouched fragment of 1952. The company is fresh, for Mr Saunders regularly changes his cast and director, but the text is Agatha Christie's expert narrative of murder in a Berkshire guest-house: a murder still an unsolved crime for an untold number of people.

Before me is the programme I stuffed carelessly into an overcoat pocket on that cold winter night in 1952. On its cover is a mousetrap upon a splash of crimson. No clues within, just details of the cast, the set (by Roger Furse), and the customary credits: an electric cleaner, an actress's 'bootees and shoes'. This was the original company, directed by Peter Cotes: Mollie Ralston, Sheila Sim; Giles Ralston, John Paul; Christopher Wren, Allan McClelland; Mrs Boyle, Mignon O'Doherty; Major Metcalf, Aubrey Dexter; Miss Casewell, Jessica Spencer; Mr Paravicini, Martin Miller; Detective Sergeant Trotter, Richard Attenborough. The people had assembled in a country manor opened as an amateurishly run guest-house. It was December. Berkshire was smothered in so fierce a blizzard that to reach Newbury one would have had to hire a sledge and huskies. Anyway, when a police officer got to Monkswell, he came on skis. Why did he come? Because there had been a murder in London, and – so he hazarded – there must soon be another at Monkswell. Unless all Berkshire hunted for its skis, the house was unapproachable; the telephone was conveniently out of order. In a closed-circle world, as impregnable as Nigger Island, somebody must die. Who? On the night I wondered why we had to assimilate so many crusts of past history, and I did question the improbability of the guest-house and its clientele. But why worry? Audiences across twenty-five years have known the answers; many thousands have yet to find out. Though cynics can laugh, and they do, their laughter is hollow (even that word is Dame Agatha's).

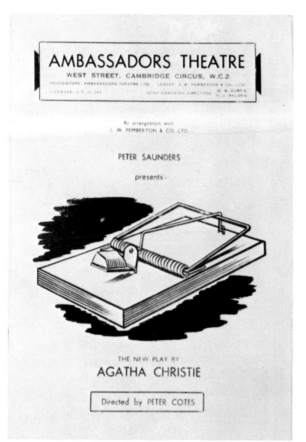

The world's longest runner:
Below: Roger Furse's set design for
the first production of *The Mousetrap*

Left: A first-night programme,
a mousetrap upon a splash of crimson
no title necessary. The production
starred Richard Attenborough as
the detective, *right*, with Sheila Sim
as Mollie Ralston, the proprietress
of the guest-house.

Overleaf: A triumph of economy, *The Mousetrap* requires only one set
and a cast of eight. The detective (Attenborough) has
just entered the closed-circle world of Monkswell Manor to
announce the news of a murder in London and the likelihood
of another at the guest-house. The trap is set.

5

Two agonies of drama criticism – much less pressing now than they were – are to describe an intimate revue from last week's unmarked programme, and to discuss almost any thriller at any time; the gentlest hint can alert a trained reader. Reviews of the later Christies were often sour; I suspected a sense of critical frustration. Not that anyone mocked the two post-*Mousetrap* plays: *Witness for the Prosecution* (1953), based on a short story, and *Spider's Web* (1954).

Witness for the Prosecution was both her craftiest and most elaborate play (not elaborate in the *Akhnaton* sense). New York, where it had 646 performances, more than in London, agreed. Its people, in the theatre, were plausible, and anyone who divined the plot from those preliminaries in the Temple could have seen through a pair of stairs and a deal door. Call it a quick flame of the Theatre Theatrical; during its two-and-a-half hours *Witness* never smouldered perilously. Leonard Vole was in the Old Bailey dock, on trial for murder, an 'intricate impeach' and a court scene as accurate as any in recollection; earlier, counsel and solicitor had debated the case in chambers; and we returned there, towards the end, for an episode in which Patricia Jessel disguised herself so surely, even reducing her height, that her mother did not recognize her. The last minutes of the piece startled me as much as a vital line from quite another context, the close of a venerable Wallace novel, *The Crimson Circle* (something, not that it matters, like 'a crimson circle ran round the neck of Derrick Yale').

Possibly chilled by its decoration, the Winter Garden, where you had to walk about a league to the front of the stalls, was not a lucky theatre. It had been long ago, with such matters as *Kissing Time*, *Kid Boots*, and *The Vagabond King*. Now *Witness for the Prosecution*, defying any hard-luck story, had an ovation comparable to the sustained hysteria after a musical. Peter Saunders said that, as Mrs Christie, overwhelmed, left her box, she whispered to him: 'It's rather fun, isn't it?' It was. Agatha Christie would not approach such success again, though she had an even longer run (774 performances to 468 for *Witness*) with *Spider's Web* in 1954.

An even-tempered writer, she was not a mercurial humorist and never given to epigram. *Spider's Web*, at the Savoy, had more genuine, counterpointing relief than in her other plays. This was, owing largely to Margaret Lockwood – technique matching technique –

SAVOY THEATRE, STRAND, W.C.2

Licensed by the Lord Chamberlain to HUGH WONTNER, M.V.O.
Proprietors SAVOY THEATRE LTD. General Manager FREDERIC [...]

Box Office Phone TEMple Bar 8888

PETER SAUNDERS presents

Margaret Lockwood

in

Agatha Christie's

SPIDER'S WEB

Directed by WALLACE DOUGLAS   Decor by MICHAEL WEIGHT

Margaret Lockwood caught up in
Spider's Web (programme, *left*),
and with the playwright at
the first night of *Towards Zero*,
a play where one critic deplorably
named the murderer in his review.

as a soaringly inventive diplomatist's wife, Clarissa Hailsham-Brown. (Clarissa was one of Mrs Christie's names.) During the first act she had murmured to herself: 'Suppose I were to find a dead body in the drawing-room? What am I going to do?' Promptly she found the body and did quite a lot, wrapping her stories round each other like layers of onion-skin while the police waited, baffled and patient. An endearing play of its school and fortified by its steely construction, it did last five minutes too long: rare in a Christie, but nobody minded.

6

Now, as a dramatist, she began a slow descent from the crest. It might be better to call this final period a sierra; among her last seven plays, four of them full-length, she could still achieve a run of 604 performances. In the background loomed *The Mousetrap*, part of the West End furniture. Established long before the so-called theatre revolution, when the English Stage Company was neither an idea nor a name, it has outlived new waves and second waves and trickling fashions.

Towards Zero (1956), first of the final group, had to be transient. Adapted (with Gerald Verner) from the novel, it opened on a late summer night at the old St James's, uncomfortable but historic, and so exasperated a critic that he named the murderer ('X did it'). Having missed the première, it was a useful test to see how a puzzle survived when one knew the crib. It managed a little better than I feared, a harmless affair, though minor Christie, and apt to be verbose. Instead of 'Wait until you leave', a character would say: 'I think you would be advised to postpone further discussion until the termination of your visit.' Old Lady Tressilian (Mrs Christie's spelling) had been battered to death at a Cornish address, Gull's Point, Saltcreek; the lethal instrument, niblick or fire-iron, was as blunt as a probing Scotland Yard superintendent was acute. Though the plot implied that Yard men might profitably take their vacations in Cornwall, I doubted the play's value as a regional advertisement.

With, for a change, a Bloomsbury setting, *Verdict* (1958) had in the programme a note on the meaning of 'amaranth', and in the play the murder of a professor's wife who suffered from a wasting disease. For once Mrs Christie composed her narrative less as a sorting-office for facts and inferences than as a play of character-conflict. Tepidly imagined, it had an irritating première; in some cue-light misunderstanding the Strand Theatre's curtain fell half a minute before it should have done, and the gallery was not too pleased. Agatha Christie, resilient as ever, took only a month (*Verdict*'s entire life) to write *The Unexpected Guest* – whereupon, just as unexpectedly, it lasted for over 600 performances. We were now in a South Wales house, near the Bristol Channel, on a night blanketed in fog, the very weather for a murderer to slip by. I had just come up from holiday at my own village, The Lizard, so one line struck me forcibly: 'I was lying awake listening to the booming of the foghorn – very depressing I always found it, sir.' The play was by no means depressing: it might have boomed into space, but Mrs Christie used the fog subtly to blind and baffle. Even if weather had cleared by the time she asked us who shot the man in the wheel-chair, we wandered in contented circles for the rest of the evening.

Serenity now for eighteen months. Then Hubert Gregg, who had directed *The Unexpected Guest* for Peter Saunders, staged *Go Back for Murder* (1960) at the same theatre, the Duchess. Founded on Mrs Christie's *Five Little Pigs*, it lacked the mettle of *Three Blind Mice*. Who poisoned the artist a generation ago? A girl from Canada, determined to prove her mother's innocence, arranges a replay sixteen years later on the scene of the crime (West of England). It was all marginal; we rarely entered the picture, for the people were as distant as the Egyptians of *Akhnaton*.

So, in December 1962, to the last of the acted Christies: a triple bill, *Rule of Three*, also at the Duchess. By then she could have echoed Matthew Arnold (that unlikely admirer of the melodrama of *The Silver King*) when he wrote:

> . . . Repeated shocks, again, again,
> Exhaust the energy of strongest souls,
> And numb the elastic powers.

Three puzzles in a night might have been uncommon *largesse*. In the event, only the first play counted, a cunning Guignol brevity: one summer afternoon in a fifth-floor Hampstead flat furnished with such trifles as a Damascus bride-chest, a Kurdish dagger, and what seemed to be a gourd from Baghdad. Sharply, claustrophobically, the plot closed in like the walls of *The Pit and the Pendulum*. Good; but the rest of the evening slid away. Mrs Christie set *Afternoon at the Seaside*, central panel of her triptych, on a crowded beach at Little Slyppynge-on-Sea. The name hinted at strain. The anecdote,

about the theft of a diamond necklace, was unexciting; and so too, until its curtain, was *The Patient*: a nursing-home, a private room, a woman paralysed from a fall over her balcony, a cross-fire of accusation, a complicated electric device, and, suddenly, a stinging last line. After more than thirty years Agatha Christie could leave her stage with honour.

7

Dame Agatha's strength in the theatre was her power of plotting. She could do most things with a body, but it became increasingly hard to animate the gap between death and revelation. Usually people and dialogue were functional, though at times, as in the whole of *Witness for the Prosecution*, in much of *The Mousetrap*, in the second

acts of *The Hollow* and *Ten Little Niggers*, in the incidental comedy of *Spider's Web*, and in *The Unexpected Guest*, the stage could flash swiftly to life. Very few detachable lines keep a play in memory; humour often stiffened to mannerism. Someone says in *Verdict*: 'I've never been to an inquest in this country. Are they always like this?' A doctor replies: 'Oh, they vary, you know; they vary.' So did the Christie plays.

That admitted, Agatha Christie had more narrative impulse than anyone of her day. Frequently her end would justify the means. She was a technician when, among critics, the word had mildewed. Our pleasure in her major puzzles was the pleasure of a testing anagram, of an exact mortise-and-tenon, of filling the space at 27 down and closing an awkward corner. In fine, the pleasure of solution, the

Opposite above : Agatha Christie at the 10th anniversary celebration party for
The Mousetrap, cutting the cake (with a little help from Sybil Thorndike)
while Peter Saunders, the play's impresario, looks on.
Above : The Mousetrap comes of age: the playwright at the 21st anniversary of the
play, with Sir Max Mallowan (centre), Peter Saunders (right) and her grandson.

answer to a precisely stated challenge. In the matter of life and death within her world of artifice, she could be past-mistress of the artificial: no leopardess, no organ at midnight, not even a vault. She failed when her heart was not with the problem (*Towards Zero*, *Go Back for Murder*, *Verdict*). When she had persuaded herself she could soon persuade others: in the period's most rubbed jargon, there might not be many 'insights', but the machine did 'work'.

Agatha Christie fortified the theatre of entertainment; she knew about plays of menace before the tag was modish. At least three of her plays should live beyond the century, and I hazard that critics then will be just as ingeniously allusive as our contemporaries. Because, in fairness, one cannot describe the plays in detail, references and analogies accumulate. In a moraine of Christie reviews I found allusions to Wilde ('This shilly-shallying with the subject is absurd'), Webster ('Their life, a general mist of error'), Sheridan ('a very pretty quarrel'), Dickens, Pinero, O'Casey, Beerbohm, Gilbert, many more: Gilbert (this was from a notice in 1951) because of the gentle milkmaid's response in *Patience* to 'O, hollow, hollow, hollow!' 'It is not a hunting-song,' exclaims Bunthorne, grieved; but what else, asked the writer, could it be in Agatha Christie? What indeed?

When, for a minute, there is silence, and argument (but not *The Mousetrap*) is over, we returned to the publicity man's jingle long ago: 'Pray don't tell them how it ends.' A dramatist who conceived so many secrets, and who kept them for so long, ought to be remembered; and I suggest, with affection, that Dame Agatha Christie will have her reward.

Philip Jenkinson
The Agatha Christie Films

AGATHA CHRISTIE was never as well served on film as her contemporary thriller writers from America. Hercule Poirot, her most filmed creation, never acquired the stature of Philip Marlowe or even Ellery Queen in his screen appearances, and of the nineteen feature films drawn from Dame Agatha's work, only a few can reasonably claim to add to the status of the author of *The Mousetrap* rather than merely draw attention to it.

Even so, these films used a wide selection of often talented film makers and represented a curious cross-section of the film styles of the half-century in which they were made.

First out was *Die Abenteuer G.m.b.H.* (*Adventure Inc.*), made by Fred Sauer in 1928 from *The Secret Adversary*. It is not surprising that Germany with its enterprising film industry and its passion for the British crime scene – Sherlock Holmes, Edgar Wallace, Jack the Ripper and Dr Crippen – should be the first country to tackle this very British writer. In the cast may be noticed Eve Gray, the heroine

Carlo Aldini and Eve Gray in *Die Abenteuer G.m.b.H* (1928),
a German production and the first adaptation of a Christie
novel (*The Secret Adversary*) for the screen.

of Dupont's English films, *Piccadilly* and *Moulin Rouge*, and Michael Rasumny, the talented comedian of later Hollywood products.

The same year saw the production of *The Passing of Mr Quinn*, made by producer-director Julius Hagen. This effort starts rather slowly, with scenes of the unpleasant Professor Appleby mistreating his wife, played by Trilby Clark; he is soon 'carrying on an intrigue' with the maid, played by Ursula Jeans. The wife is so upset that she sends a letter to the wealthy tenant of the nearby house stating that she could kill the husband, who sure enough is poisoned. The wealthy neighbour and the doctor, played by the film's star Stewart Rome, come to her aid. All is resolved in one of the flashback disclosures characteristic of the crime films of this period. This was derived from *The Coming of Mr Quin* (with only one 'n' incidentally).

In 1931 Hagen produced *Alibi*, derived from *The Murder of Roger Ackroyd*. This was directed by Leslie Hiscott, who had scripted *The Passing of Mr Quinn*. The film began a series in which Austin Trevor played Hercule Poirot. Trevor, who may be glimpsed in the English films of Korda and Hitchcock, was a competent actor but was totally

Above : Austin Trevor (centre, wearing hat) in *Alibi* (1931), one of a series of films in which he played Poirot. The clean-shaved Trevor was never the likeliest personification of the detective, and was overshadowed by Charles Laughton's contemporary stage characterization in the part.

Opposite : Stewart Rome, the star of *The Passing of Mr Quinn* (1928) a title which intriguingly amended that of the original story, *The Coming of Mr Quin*.

overshadowed by a contemporary stage characterization by Charles Laughton in the part. Trevor did not attempt any kind of character performance – unlike his successors – and later commented that he thought he'd been given the role because he'd played a Frenchman in another film. One writer trying to puff interest in a later entry in the series pointed out that 'the detective is described by the authoress as an elderly man with an egg-shaped head and bristling moustache. Austin Trevor is a good-looking young man and clean-shaven into the bargain!'

In *Alibi*, Poirot was called in to investigate the suicide of a widow loved by the well-to-do, but unpopular, village squire. Trevor was well received in the lead but the women in the film (Elizabeth Allen and Clare Greet) were less sympathetically reviewed and the standard detective format of deduction and revelation was followed.

Director Hiscott managed to keep things moving in his first film but after this his second entry, *Black Coffee*, was considered an anti-climax. The stage origins showed clearly, notably in the murder scene where Sir Claude Amory, played by C. V. France, rounded up his house guests and demanded that whoever stole his secret formula

replace it on the table when he turned out the lights! Chief among the suspects were daughter-in-law Adrianne Allen and son Philip Strange, because she was being blackmailed for her guilty secret – her father was a famous Italian spy. Doctor Dino Galvani was responsible for this piece of evil doing, but Trevor as Poirot outsmarted the murderer, feigning drinking poisoned coffee. A passing word of praise should go to the camerawork of William Luff and Sidney Blythe – the latter one of the better British craftsmen of the day, who shortly after gave up movies to open a pub.

The cycle halted with *Lord Edgware Dies*, directed by Henry Edwards from the novel of the same name (called *Thirteen at Dinner* in America), once more for producer Julius Hagen. In this thriller Trevor as Poirot finds the identity of the murderer of the husband of the attractive but vain American actress, played by Jane Carr. The film was well enough acted, ingenious and spaced with several more murders, but by 1934 audiences were finding these entertainments talk-bound and the literal adaptation made one contemporary reviewer dismiss the film as 'just another conventional mystery play'.

These films were played within the conventions of the indigenous British film industry of their day with plaster faked timber country houses, theatrical devices in both writing and staging and the ubiquitous 'silly ass' comics – played by John Deverell in *Alibi* or Richard Cooper in *Black Coffee*. Even the means of murder – hyoscine in the coffee – dates the films and the villain referring to Poirot as a 'cunning swine' as his most strong invective never quite rang with conviction. Like most of their contemporaries these British quota fillers seem to have totally vanished but one is bound to record that they are undoubtedly among the lesser of the cinema's losses.

The first film that anyone – other than a veteran of habitual movie-going in the thirties – might reasonably be expected to have seen is the 1937 *Love from a Stranger*, derived from the play written by Hitchcock villain Frank Vosper, based on Mrs Christie's short story 'Philomel Cottage'. Here the director was an old Hollywood hand, Roland V. Lee, whose output, while uneven, contained several films of considerable interest: *Zoo in Budapest*, *Cardinal Richelieu* and *Captain Kidd*. He at least might have been expected to impose an assured film style upon the material but sadly this hope was not fulfilled; the talk-dominated form of the play producing an unconvincing and sluggish film.

Austin Trevor was again Poirot in *Black Coffee*,
a film that never really escaped its stage origins.
(Left to right: Trevor, Adrienne Allen,
Dino Galliene, Richard Cooper.)

The most interesting element was naturally the central performance of Basil Rathbone as Gerald, the fortune-hunter with a smooth line in murdering rich women. Rathbone was always a striking if unsubtle performer and even under-controlled here, gets all the attention away from Ann Harding's Carol, whom he meets when inspecting the flat she puts up for sale after a lottery win. Soon, however, there are sinister happenings in the cellar of the country cottage in which the newly married couple settle. His heart condition brings the doctor, and with Miss Harding's ex-suitor hovering about it's not long until the photo of the bearded murderer, who strangely resembles the bridegroom, comes to light.

The films most interesting sequence is the climax, where Rathbone's intention to murder Harding in the deserted cottage becomes clear and she has only her wits for protection. Pretending she has poisoned his coffee as part of *her* succession of murders she works on Rathbone's weak heart and in an audaciously conceived sequence he strides back and forwards about her, trying to reassure himself and master his condition, towering over Harding and the camera.

The subject was again filmed as *Love from a Stranger* (*A Stranger Passes* in the UK where the Rathbone film was still occasionally shown) in 1947, for Eagle Lion – an independent Hollywood company of the time. The script owed little to the adaptation by Frances Marion for the earlier film. (She had written, among others, *The Big House.*) The new version was one of a number of film scripts which Philip Macdonald, himself an established thriller writer, was then preparing. The Jacques Tourneur–Ray Milland English film *Circle of Danger* was, however, a much better example of his skill.

In the remake, Cecily Harrington wins the fifty thousand pound Calcutta Sweepstakes and into her life comes a charming, sinister new husband who proves to have the same dreadful secret. Even with an attempt to provide a more actionful climax this production was destroyed by its cheapness, its obvious studio setting – noticeable even in the exteriors – and poor playing. Time had not treated kindly the appearance of Sylvia Sidney since her great thirties performances, and John Hodiak made little headway in replacing his characteristic clean-cut GI style with the more sombre character he attempted here or in *Desert Fury* and *Somewhere in the Night*. Richard Whorf's disappointing direction must largely be blamed. Indeed, the only participant to come out of the production with any credit was veteran

cameraman Tony Gaudio, who held attention with his suggestion of electrical storms and the lamplit, remote house where 'something nasty is going on in the cellar'.

It is to be regretted that these projects did not attract talent of the calibre involved in such similar films as *Gaslight* and *Night Must Fall*, both using popular melodramas as their source material. *Love from a Stranger*, however, was not the most filmed of the Agatha Christie subjects. This distinction undoubtedly goes to *Ten Little Niggers*, of which the first official version, also called *And Then There Were None*, was made in Hollywood in 1945, two years before *A Stranger Passes*.

This remarkable film is one of the most successful attempts to put its author on the screen and deserves serious attention. Entrusting the direction to the French director René Clair was a curious decision on the face of it. Throughout the thirties Clair had been regarded as the leading European light comedy talent in film-making. While many of his films do not justify the awe in which they were once held, all have his special elaborate visual gags, such as the wedding party

Love From a Stranger (1937) was derived from the short story *Philomel Cottage*. Here a villainous Basil Rathbone, as the fortune-hunting Gerald, attempts to murder Ann Harding.

circle kissing one another, shot straight downwards for *Italian Straw Hat*, the rooftop chase involving an escaped lunatic, the police, the head of the underworld and the lottery winner's creditors in *Le Million*, or the suicide's gun flung on the gaming table in the state where the barter economy operates, thus winning the player a stack of pistols in *The Last Millionaire*.

One would have to search way back into the silent period and films like *Prey to the Wind* to find a straightforward mystery movie in Clair's work. However, the audacity of choosing him to make the Christie subject paid off remarkably. The film was cast with some of the best character players in Hollywood – most gifted comics like Roland Young, Mischa Auer, Sir C. Aubrey Smith – and backed with some of the best technicians, designer Ernest Fegte of *The General Died at Dawn* fame and René Hubert, who costumed the Korda films, among them. In these hands the story's more macabre elements were kept well in hand and the unexpected casting of these assorted comedy talents in apparently straight parts upset the audience's anticipation and helped the suspense.

Possibly the only overt trace of the Clair style was in the through-the-key-holes sequence where the wary survivors watch one another. Elsewhere one notices such intriguing devices as the mysterious figure, identified by a cat, long before Welles's *The Third Man*; particularly memorable was the match-lit confrontation between Walter Huston's Dr Armstrong and Barry Fitzgerald's Judge Quinncannon, when the power fails in the deserted mansion to which the ten little Niggers have been invited. These two superb performers carefully assessing one another in a situation where each is in peril of his life is Agatha Christie and Hollywood of its great period at their very best.

Clair's Hollywood films varied both in their success and their quality, but the widely held belief that they fell below the level of his European work is totally bogus and with *And Then There Were None*, his last American film, he achieved a situation where he was able to use the enormous resources of the American industry to their fullest extent.

The story was to be filmed twice more. The 1966 version was set in the Austrian Alps and made for Harry Allen Towers by George Pollock – veteran of the Miss Marple adventures at that stage. The film also assembled and largely squandered the talents of a gifted

Arguably the best of all
the Christie adaptations
for the screen was
René Clair's *Ten Little
Niggers* (US: *And Then
There Were None*) made
in 1945. Partly this was
because of its comparative
faithfulness to
the author's intentions
both in the setting
(*right*) and the suspense, as
in the confrontation (*above*)
between Walter Huston's
Dr Armstrong and
Barry Fitzgerald's
Judge Quincannon (seated).

cast, notably Stanley Holloway as the overbearing William Blore, Dennis Price as Dr Armstrong, Leo Genn in the C. Aubrey Smith character, General Mandrake, and the menacing German actor Mario Adorf as the butler. Poor Daliah Lavi was not attractively photographed but Shirley Eaton, her career revived by *Goldfinger*, got an unusually provocative love scene (an innovation for the Agatha Christie films) with Hugh O'Brian, fresh from being TV's Wyatt Earp. The film's many murders are free of gore, however, and while the death of the brunette (as if Christie victims were colour-coded) and the wandering about the deserted snow-country hotel recall the Marple films, the production values are closer to those of the cheap Merton Park thrillers. The film's one innovation is its most interesting element. Before the final revelation we have a 'Who-done-it' break – a sort of composite of the flashback explanation of the thirties detective films and William Castle's *Fright Break*. In this, the murders are

Dinner for eight in René Clair's version
of *Ten Little Niggers* (*left*), and the equivalent
scene (*above*) in the 1966 *Ten Little Indians*, which
not only evasively altered the title but also
changed the setting to the Austrian Alps.

recapped against the clock while the audience is supposed to ponder
the solution.

Following the success of *Murder on the Orient Express*, Towers
dusted off the script of this film and proceeded to make it again as
And Then There Were None (*Ten Little Indians* in the States), in 1974.
This time the events take place at the Shah Abah Hotel in Isfahan,
Persia, and the colour photography is the film's greatest asset. Where
Marrianne Hoppe had died in the ski-lift crash in the 1966 film,
Maria Rohm is executed traditionally by strangulation on one of the
pillars of the ruins, which Oliver Reed described as 'about two
thousand five hundred years old – give or take a century'.

Once more an intriguing cosmopolitan cast is assembled and used
to little effect, with the European players poorly post-synchronized.
Charles Aznavour's cabaret star does one of his own numbers where
Fabian's Mike Raven the pop star,(!) had had to content himself with

very ordinary material, but the match-lit dialogue – here between Herbert Lom and Richard Attenborough – is totally outclassed by the Clair film. However, fifties sex-kitten Elke Sommer still shows a welcome willingness to discard her black blouse and Morricone's conductor, Bruno Nicolai, doing one of his imitation Morricone scores, is better than the routine music of the earlier remake.

In charge of this last version was Peter Collinson who once looked like the hope of the new British films of the late sixties but only with *The Italian Job* delivered. His set pieces are pretty tame – the camera circling the dinner table with the guests facing the ten ceramic Indians, Gert Frobe's dubbed 'Martino' echoing through the empty cellar or Richard Attenborough's red-faced death. The identity of the mysterious Mr U. N. Owen, so puzzling to a decade of bit players, is hardly concealed; we all recognize the tape-recorded voice of Orson Welles instantly.

The 1974 version (*And Then There Were None*, again!) assembled a cosmopolitan cast in a hotel in Persia. Hugh Lombard (Oliver Reed) and Vera Clyde (Elke Sommer) look on shocked as Mr Martino (Alberto de Mendoza) discovers the body of his wife (Maria Rohm), strangled on one of the pillars of the ruins; her counterpart in the 1966 film had died in a ski-lift crash.

While these are the official versions of the Christie story they are far from the only attempt at filming it. *Ten Little Niggers* has joined *The Cat and the Canary* or *The Maltese Falcon* as one of the standard movie plots. It cropped up again as recently as *Breakheart Pass* and the reason that James Garner gave for leaving the enormously popular Maverick series was that the producers had made him do the same script five times and it wasn't original even then. It had been *Ten Little Indians*.

The first film to be made from an Agatha Christie original in the ten years after *A Stranger Passes* was an adaptation of her enormously successful stage version of *Witness for the Prosecution*.

The film had a certain suspense element outside of its subject in posing the question of how a 1957 audience would react to what was basically a thirties courtroom murder mystery. The author could scarcely have been better served. Billy Wilder, already the director of *Lost Weekend*, *Sunset Boulevard* and *The Seven Year Itch*, had been asked to read the script and give an opinion for producer Arthur Hornblow, for whom Wilder had often written and once directed in his early years. Instead of an outside nomination, Wilder proposed himself as director and with him came an ambitious and very individual two-hour adaptation.

Wilder's previous film *Love in the Afternoon* had been made in Europe and hadn't performed all that well, so for this he installed himself on Goldwyn Studio's Stage Four. However, the previous film's famous art director Alexander Trauner was in charge, so the £75,000 Old Bailey replica and the film's other décors were executed with great imagination. One remembers the sinister narrow corridored view of the prison or the sound stage Oxford Street, in which the London buses are only seen as reflections in the shop windows. The film's picture of then-contemporary London might not convince but it was the same remove from reality as the courtroom theatricals of the text.

Black and white photography had seemed doomed with the arrival of wide screen but films like *Witness for the Prosecution* reprieved it for another twenty years with Russell Harlan's lighting etching the scenes like a steel engraving. The other technical credits were also assured but the film's great joy was its casting, with Charles Laughton's ailing, histrionic barrister superbly wringing laughs out of the leading part, which Francis L. Sullivan had played straight on the stage. With

Billy Wilder's 1957 film
of *Witness for the Prosecution* proved to be a great
success, not least because
of the by-play between
Elsa Lanchester's
Nurse Plimsol (*right*) and
Charles Laughton's ailing
and histrionic barrister,
and because of the
imaginative décor of
the Old Bailey replica
in which he performed
(*below*).
Left: Marlene Dietrich
being challenged by her
defendant husband,
Tyrone Power, in a
setting far removed from
the wartime Germany
where they had met
(*below left*).

superb control Marlene Dietrich made the part of the client's German wife one of the cinema's great virtuoso performances, a role not too distant from the one she had played under Wilder in *A Foreign Affair*. John Williams, Henry Daniel and Torin Thatcher made up the perfect team of gentleman lawyer foils and playing the part of the nurse for laughs gave great range to Elsa Lanchester. Even Tyrone Power's ageing juvenile features with 'Captain Marvel' eyebrows were perfectly suited to the part of Lennard Vole, accused of murdering the rich woman whose recent will turned out to be in his favour.

Wilder made the comedy material very much his own with scenes like Laughton's Sir Wilfred snatching the calcium shot-needle, which Lanchester's Nurse Plimsol brandishes as she descends in the chair lift, and using it to pierce his forbidden cigar, or his comment as they lay out his medication that 'The judge will be asking for a saliva test'. There's Power nervously offering a light to Dietrich after he has given her a choice between cigarettes and chewing gum and she has taken the latter. The details are superbly handled, as with the incriminating marriage certificate followed round the court till Laughton waves it aside as *his* surprise evidence will be passed about in the final stages of the action, and the cook's nervousness with the microphone which contrasts with Dietrich's glacial calm. The film craft is exceptional with the framing carefully excluding scene-stealing Laughton from the wide shot in which Power gives his testimony, or the montage of London location scenes which is still in progress over the actual witness for the prosecution line.

Indeed these great talents at first seem to be wasted on old-fashioned material – old jokes like Sir Wilfred's 'What war?' jibe, or his 'I'm surprised that women's hats don't provoke more murders', devices like the monocle shining in the face during the interrogation which Dietrich disarms by pulling the blind, or the time lapse indicated by the disappearance of the pills which Laughton has to take. The social comment is thin as in the reference to 'those foreign wives'. However, the element of the law-as-theatre has been introduced with asides like 'There's no disgrace in being arrested Mr Vole' or the audience craning forward to hear the plea – and soon we have the mutter that runs under the exchange about perjury with the jury turning to Dietrich. Gradually these elements become more pointed, as with Laughton's superbly delivered reference to 'the suspense of this horror fiction' as he describes the damning testimony.

The stage is being set for the quadruple twist of the authoress's ending which, twenty years after the film was made, still wrings spontaneous applause from the audience, even for those already familiar with the ingenuity with which it was conceived. There is not only the suspense of the verdict and of Sir Wilfred's health – 'Let's hope we shall both survive' – but the question of the true sequence of events left to be determined, and beyond that the vindication of Sir Wilfred's position and the English legal system, so fascinating to world audiences from John Galsworthy through to *QB VII* with its outrage at the 'You have made a mockery of English law' sub-climax.

By removing any exact depiction of time and place and emphasizing the theatrical effect of the work, Wilder and his associates produced what was certainly the most remarkable film to be made from Agatha Christie material. Its continuing popularity is testimony to that.

It is then surprising that the only film to follow up on this surge of enthusiasm was made three years later, the very minor *The Spider's Web*. The Danzigers were an English company specializing in low-budget supporting films.

The Spider's Web was an attempt at a more ambitious production using colour and better-known players. Director Godfrey Grayson was one of the more skilled members of their stable and had shown a light touch in some of his smaller films. Unfortunately, the production was misconceived and passed without notice or effect.

Glynis Johns and John Justin are the Hailsham-Browns, a diplomat and his wife based in the country house, Copplestone Court. While Henry is off collecting a foreign dignitary, Clarissa finds the body of the blackmailing husband of Henry's former wife. This character played by Ferdy Mayne has threatened to take away little Pippa, the daughter of the first marriage. In a panic, Clarissa calls her guardian Sir Roland (Roly) Delahaye, a part which brings out thirties British comedy star, Jack Hulbert, in a comeback somewhat less dazzling than his old contemporary Jack Buchanan had just enjoyed with *The Bandwagon*. Roly's plans to shift the body into the conveniently nearby woods are frustrated when the police, who have been alerted by a phone call, arrive and the further ploy of hiding it behind a secret panel is in turn upset by the local nosyparker, Miss Peake, played by Hulbert's long-standing partner Cicely Courtneidge. The body of course keeps on vanishing and reappearing, once in Roly's bedroom, before the murderer is unmasked and life at Copplestone Court can resume.

Despite the discouraging example of *The Spider's Web*, the Christie subjects were in for another burst of activity. MGM had possessed a studio in Britain at Borehamwood since the immediate pre-war days of American interest in British production. In order to keep the complex in operation – one of the last in Britain to employ contract technicians – the company made, in the sixties, a number of medium budget black and white co-features with British comics like Terry-Thomas and Spike Milligan. With a five-week schedule, these films were often made by name technicians filling in between more ambitious productions and regarding them largely as a holiday.

The first of these was the Agatha Christie Miss Marple mystery, the 1961 *Murder She Said*, based on *4.50 From Paddington*, and starring Margaret Rutherford. This unique British comedienne had contributed her talent to several decades of British cinema, occasionally in films like *Blithe Spirit* but mostly in vehicles that were unworthy of her. She was to celebrate her eightieth birthday on the set of *Murder Ahoy* and to win an Oscar for her appearance in *The VIPs* shortly after, and she remained an immense asset in the part of Miss Marple. The release of *Murder She Said* coincided with a boom in an American interest in British eccentricity and it was decided to turn the film into a series.

Unfortunately, these films were not to use the Rutherford potential as they might, being patterned on the Hollywood detective series of the forties and working for an uninvolving suspense rather than comedy. Further, the age of Margaret Rutherford and her contemporaries whom she always worked into the productions (her husband, the amiable Stringer Davies was a regular character) meant modifications to the shooting methods, such as breaking up the longer speeches more than they might normally have been in order to make memorizing them more simple.

Director George Pollock, who had assisted David Lean on *Brief Encounter*, was as much involved in engineering devices like this as in developing the suspense and comedy elements. Three of the four films of the series were written by the team of David Pursall and Jack Seddon and the series was constructed very much to formula, with a murder attracting Miss Marple's attention and bringing her into contact with some juveniles and some name character comics until enough of them got murdered for the guilty parties to be singled out by an ingenious trap set by Miss Marple to the bemusement of Charles Tingwell's Inspector Craddock. The films had sequences of talk-bound deduction and all featured long scenes of the innocent parties thanking Miss Marple for her efforts in clearing their name. The few laughs came from Margaret Rutherford's appearance in a variety of curious outfits or gamely undertaking such enterprises as doing the twist or fencing under the supervision of an Olympic champion. Still, Ron Goodwin's theme was catchy and enjoyed a certain popularity in its day.

Murder She Said, made in 1961, enjoyed a remarkably strong cast, including of all people Arthur Kennedy, with James Robertson Justice, Muriel Pavlow, Ronald Howard and Thorley Walters. It is the best Rutherford performance in the role and significantly is one of Dame Agatha's murder-on-a-train mysteries. *Murder at the Gallop* (scripted by one James Cavenaugh) starts off with the Agatha Christie preoccupation with cats once again and soon Miss Marple is investigating the death of a recluse and snooping about The Gallop, a riding school run by Robert Morley's Hector Enderby with Flora Robson looking on suspiciously.

Murder Most Foul (1964) starts with Miss Marple's disagreement with her fellow jurors over a young prisoner's guilt and soon finds her enrolled in Ron Moody's local 'Cosgood Players'. The final film, *Murder Ahoy*, has her analysing poison samples which send her off to upset the smooth running of Captain Lionel Jeffries' training ship.

The series had proved modestly popular and the contact with the author, who took an interest in the productions, continued. (When Mrs Christie wondered if she could have the naval gun mountings used in *Murder Ahoy* for an antique cannon she owned, one studio executive suggested she must be tired of firing from the hip.)

It was hoped that a film would be made from *The A.B.C. Murders* – a Hercule Poirot adventure. Director Seth Holt and star Zero Mostel were retained and an adaptation made, which included a bedroom scene for Poirot. Dame Agatha was not amused and the production was abandoned on what was to have been the first day of shooting.

The film did finally emerge in a Pursall and Seddon adaptation with Tony Randall directed by Frank Tashlin. Where the bulk of the previous films had used comedy business and atmospheric filmic passages to space out the Christie-style dialogue, Tashlin was a one

time Bugs Bunny director and talent behind the delirious Jayne Mansfield comedies *The Girl Can't Help It* and *Oh for a Man*, and his style of film making was quick-fire visual comedy. Thus his stamp is very definitely on *The Alphabet Murders* as the film was finally known. Things move from a striking opening with the aquatic clown killed (in the deserted swimming baths) by a poisoned dart, which goes from the close up of the dart striking his neck to the shot of his feet-upwards form falling away into the water. This surreal element is carefully emphasized with the shots of Anita Ekberg on horseback galloping through Kensington Gardens and a succession of killings, all with alphabetically succeeding initials. Soon we are at King's Cross where a Scotland-bound express carries the coffin containing the body of Sir Carmichael Clark. The comedy element is mainly in the hands of Robert Morley's Hastings, a British undercover man whose wife thinks he's something in Agriculture and Fisheries and who keeps on getting his bowler-hatted dignity bundled into car boots as he attempts to protect Randall's straight-played Poirot. Notice among the support Austin Trevor, our original Poirot. *The*

As a one-time Bugs Bunny director, Frank Tashlin was not the most obvious choice to direct *The Alphabet Murders*. However, the result was a stylish and amusing film, with Robert Morley's bowler-hatted Hastings (on the left) comically attempting to protect Tony Randall's Poirot.

Alphabet Murders is certainly the most stylish and amusing of the Agatha Christie 'B' movies and one can only regret that a series was not forthcoming.

After the George Pollock *Ten Little Indians*, there was another pause to the 1972 *Endless Night*. Written and directed by Sidney Gilliat, the film echoes the work he did with Frank Launder in the forties, such as Alistair Sim and Trevor Howard in *Green for Danger* or Howard in *I See A Dark Stranger*. Some of the more firmly entrenched British technicians were backed by a score from Bernard Herrman whom the producers obviously hoped would give the film the Hitchcock sound and emphasize the overtones of *Psycho* they were striving for.

Hayley Mills is the rich girl who marries Hywel Bennett and from the moment Britt Ekland appears as the old friend whom the groom can't abide, the outcome is obvious. Per Oscarson, the remarkable Swedish actor, was doing a few English language films at this stage (*Dandy in Aspic* dates from this period), and as the architect friend who tries to ward off the disaster he makes considerable impression, though his character is devalued by the grotesque house which he is supposed to have created for the couple. George Sanders, in one of his last performances, also suffers from an incomprehensible characterization further weakened by poor post-synchronization.

The attempts to up-date the style with a little tame sex and some non-time-sequence editing make less impression than Harry Waxman's vivid colour photography and the Herrmann score. Appealing Hayley Mills's career had wilted with the declining British film industry and the attempt to turn her long-running partner Bennett into a new 'menace' star was no more successful than those with John Hodiak.

This brings us to 1974 and *Murder on the Orient Express*. The most ambitious British film of its day, its enormous success was a considerable embarrassment to EMI, then talking of cutting back their commitment to the unprofitable British film industry. One of the author's most celebrated and unfathomable mysteries, this Poirot adventure had long defied adaptation. Censorship alone would have frustrated any accurate rendition until the seventies. As we have seen, from the 1940s onwards, Agatha Christie adaptations have attempted to up-date their material with humour. Paul Dehn's screenplay offered the material perfectly straight, and director Sidney

Lumet used this to fashion what may well be the peak achievement of the seventies nostalgia craze. Lumet saw the film as another great train melodrama in the tradition of *The Lady Vanishes* and *Shanghai Express* and certainly its set piece is the arrival at the steam-wreathed railway station of the dazzling cast and the rhythmically edited departure of the train, headed by its massive valve-geared locomotive.

Lumet had made it a policy to alternate safer commercial subjects like *The Anderson Tapes* with more challenging material such as *The Offence*, both with Sean Connery. Sometimes his safe films failed and occasionally his difficult ones were very successful, but not having had a hit since *Serpico*, he badly needed one to ensure the high output which made him one of the last of the great American film-makers. This production was played safe with a big budget, lavish production, alternating lush period studio work with authentic snowscape locations and, particularly, filling all the parts with superb and famous players.

Probably the film's greatest joy is watching these enormous talents competing with one another. Albert Finney is buried in make-up and enjoyably coasts as Poirot, but Richard Widmark is suitably abrasive as the victim. Michael York and Jacqueline Bisset manage not to be obliterated in the thankless parts of the young married aristocrats and they are surrounded by the superb gallery of gargoyles made up of Lumet regulars, Martin Balsam as the railway official, Anthony Perkins doing Norman Bates yet again, and particularly Sean Connery, the director's regular star who manages to draw attention away from even this prestigious company. Lauren Bacall as the American matron plays opposite Widmark, with the superb and so often wasted Wendy Hiller as the countess, Rachel Roberts as her maid, Vanessa Redgrave as the lady with the husband, the deliriously anti-type casting of Ingrid Bergman as the lumpen nurse and up-staging them all because the audience is kept waiting for his big moment which he discreetly withholds – John Gielgud as the Jeeves character. Jean-Pierre Cassel is suitably inconspicuous and the featured players also would have drawn comment in any other production – Colin Blakely, George Coulouris and Denis Quilley.

Richard Williams's titles (one of his few non-comic ventures like *Charge of the Light Brigade*) set up the kidnapping and murder of the child of the rich family in impeccable period detail and soon Poirot finds himself on the Orient Express with this bizarre cross-section of

Even small parts in the 1974 *Murder on the Orient Express* were filled
by famous players, and the authentic snowscape locations and lavish
production values made it the most ambitious British film of its day.
Above : The train thunders across Europe on its three-day journey to Calais.
On board, Poirot (Albert Finney), Signor Bianchi (Martin Balsam) and
Dr Constantine (George Coulouris) survey the victim's body (below).

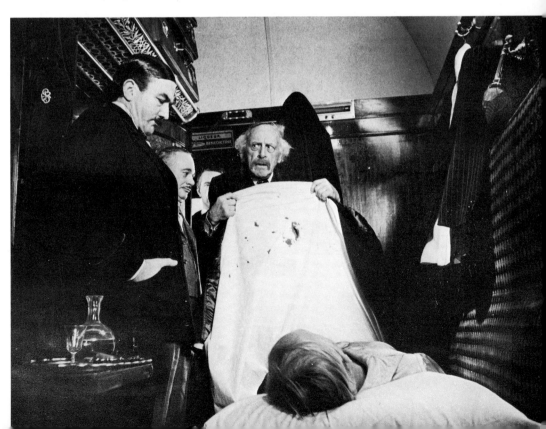

The vintage Christie climax:
the murder on the Orient Express
is solved (*above*) as the suspects –
isolated in the snow-bound
train – listen intently to
Poirot's conclusions.

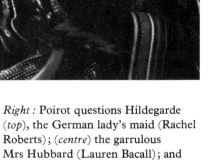

Right : Poirot questions Hildegarde
(*top*), the German lady's maid (Rachel
Roberts); (*centre*) the garrulous
Mrs Hubbard (Lauren Bacall); and
Count Andrenyi (Michael York) (*bottom*)
about a grease-spot on his passport.

humanity, all of whom appear to have some connection with this earlier event. There follows the murder and their isolation in the snowbound train. I personally value the film more for its little touches – Vanessa Redgrave's coquettish wink or Widmark brusquely pushing aside the delicate flower arrangement – than for the suspense of the approaching snow-plough which will free the train, and by consequence, the murderer. While it is a delight to watch, the film yet again sinks under the sheer weight of words, with Finney/Poirot's final double unravelling of the mystery totally uninvolving – even with its flashback visualization. There has been talk of a new Poirot series from this stable but Finney, one of the most serious and most wasted of British actors, has proved reluctant to spend more of his career padded and brilliantined. He still remembers the waste of his charming film as director, *Charlie Bubbles*, and tends to concentrate on the theatre which can regrettably be neither preserved nor widely seen.

Murder on the Orient Express showed in a spectacular fashion that the Agatha Christie magic could be made to work on film, and that attempts to dilute or update it showed little understanding of its nature. However impatient we may become with silly-ass lounge lizards, murders at the vicarage and blundering police inspectors unable to detect the exotic poison in the coffee, Agatha Christie's craftmanship will still find a public who delight in matching their imagination with one of her precisely engineered plots. Many more serious writers cannot claim a body of film work that contains titles as impressive as the 1945 *And Then There Were None*, *Witness for the Prosecution* and *Murder on the Orient Express*.

William Weaver
Music and Mystery

IN GENERAL, the arts do not come off well in the novels of Agatha Christie. Her painters, for example, are few and usually unpleasant or feckless. The best of the lot, from an artistic point of view, was no doubt Amyas Crale, posthumous protagonist of *Five Little Pigs* (America's *Murder in Retrospect*); several reputable observers – including Hercule Poirot himself – testify to the power of Crale's work; but as a human being, he was far from admirable, bearing, in his unlikeable aspects, a strong resemblance to Augustus John. There are painters, too, in *After the Funeral* (*Funerals Are Fatal*), daubers and incompetent. Only the sculptor Henrietta Savernake, in *The Hollow* (*Murder after Hours*), has both talent and a certain spiky charm, along with a deep, if reticent, humanity. But she, too, can be ruthless when it comes to her art.

Literature fares a bit better. There are several untalented and unsuccessful writers around (one in *The Crooked House*, for example); but in compensation there is Miss Marple's clever nephew Raymond West, whose novels – odd as his aunt finds them – allow him to live on an elegant scale and be generous not only to Aunt Jane (giving her a Caribbean holiday) but also to others in need, like the young heroine of the final Marple book. And, of course, there is the delightful Mrs Ariadne Oliver, Mrs Christie's wry self-caricature, warm and engaging as a person and obviously a success with her Frankenstein-monster, the Finnish detective.

The theatre gave Mrs Christie a number of characters; but again, few are sympathetic, and at least one – Charles Cartwright in *Three Act Tragedy* (*Murder in Three Acts*) – is doubly guilty, of bigamy and murder. Actors make natural suspects, if not natural criminals; and many a Christie figure in the past engaged in amateur theatricals or was perhaps a bit too brilliant in the OUDS. In the early *The Man in the Brown Suit* there is a wicked prima ballerina, and there is a reference to the Russian ballet in *The Mystery of the Blue Train*, while in the short story 'The Arcadian Deer' (one of *The Labours of Hercules*) the great Katrina's love for a garage mechanic is reminiscent of the real-life story of Karsavina, who married a racing driver. In any case, we seldom see dancers dancing, nor do we hear their music.

We know, from her rare interviews, that Agatha Christie liked music. As a young girl, she studied voice in Paris; and she had ambitions of becoming a concert pianist. But in the books of Agatha Christie music occupies a strange, ambivalent position.

As a girl Agatha Christie had considered becoming
a concert pianist, but her music master had told her
that she was too nervous to contemplate playing
in public. Nevertheless, music was a lifelong
interest, and she continued to play privately
at Greenway House and elsewhere.

Superficially, it seems absent. But under the surface, it is there. Chiefly music takes the form of nursery rhymes. Seven books have quotations from such rhymes for their titles, and the American Christie scholar G. C. Ramsey gives the tunes (some apparently sung to him by the author herself) in an appendix to his *Agatha Christie, Mistress of Mystery*. But nursery rhymes or old songs crop up also elsewhere, and in significant ways. In the very first Christie, *The Mysterious Affair at Styles*, Russian folk songs are mentioned. Kirsten, the Scandinavian murderess, in *Ordeal by Innocence*, has a song she sings, a wistful tune that recurs like a leitmotif and explains much about her character. Poirot shows interest in music. In *Cards on the Table* he 'hums a tune', but in *One, Two, Buckle My Shoe* (*The Patriotic Murders*) he actually sings and, in doing so, finds the key to the puzzle: '. . . I had my first glimmer of the truth. I was in church at the time, and singing a verse of a psalm. It spoke of a snare laid with cords . . .' Again in *The A.B.C. Murders* Poirot sings a World War I song (having previously, in the same book, compared himself to a prima donna). Poirot evinces a taste for opera in *Lord Edgware Dies* (*Thirteen at Dinner*), in which he actually puts a rose between his lips and explains to the bewildered Hastings: 'I had a fancy to pretend I was Carmen.' Hastings, incidentally, seems virtually unmusical, but he does reveal (in *The Big Four*) that he has at least heard of Handel's *Largo*. Untypically, Hastings marries an artist – or rather, an artiste, the acrobat Cinderella – but after marrying her and settling in South America, he makes suspiciously frequent trips to Europe. Perhaps Cinderella turned nasty when taken away from her art.

In *They Do It With Mirrors* (*Murder With Mirrors*) Miss Marple speaks of having been to the opera. Was this a taste acquired during her education in Italy (mentioned in the same book)? Perhaps her Italian school was like Miss Pope's establishment in 'The Girdle of Hyppolita' (another story in *The Labours of Hercules*), as described by its headmistress: 'We specialize here, M. Poirot, in Art and Music. The girls are taken to the Opera . . . The very best masters come here to instruct them in music, singing, and painting.' Miss Marple keeps a critical eye on the music situation in St Mary Mead, where the position of organist is clearly not an enviable one. In one of her *Thirteen Problems* (1932), Miss Marple remarks of an older man: 'Gentlemen of that age are sometimes very peculiar where young girls are concerned. Our last organist – but there, I mustn't talk scandal.' The village obviously had bad luck with its organists, since in *4.50 From Paddington* (*What Mrs McGillicuddy Saw!*), twenty-five years later, Miss Marple reports a 'general distrust of the new organist'.

Operas crop up here and there, sometimes in unexpected situations. The stolid Major Blunt, in *The Murder of Roger Ackroyd*, in a rather Marple-like way, finds an opera situation to compare to an event in his current life: 'Remember the Johnny who sold his soul to the devil? In return for being made young again? There's an opera about it.' The novel appeared in 1926, and it is interesting to speculate as to which production of *Faust* the major attended. Given his age, it could have been during the Hammerstein season at Covent Garden 1911–12, or more likely, during the 1919 Beecham summer season, with the Belgian tenor Fernand Ansseau as Faust and Melba as Marguerite.

A few pages after his reference to *Faust*, Major Blunt shows even more astonishing operatic knowledge. A piece of jewellery has been thrown into a pond, and clever Flora says: 'Perhaps it's a crown . . . like the one Melisande saw in the water.'

'Melisande . . . she's in an opera, isn't she?'

And Blunt explains his knowledge: 'People take me sometimes . . .' He adds a philistine comment, unfortunately fairly typical of Christie characters: 'Funny idea of pleasure – worse racket than the natives make with their tom-toms.'

Racket? In *Faust* perhaps. But in *Pelléas*? We can guess, in any event, that the major attended one of the *Pelléas* performances conducted just after the war by Percy Pitt, with Edvina, Royer, Maguenat, and Huberdeau. These were in 1920. Or, in 1924, he could have heard a more modest production by the BNOC at His Majesty's. His friends made a strange choice for their non-operatic guest.

Faust appears elsewhere. In *Cat Among the Pigeons* (1959) the schoolgirls have been 'taken to Covent Garden to hear *Faust* last week'. Here we have the sort of blunder one might expect from Ariadne Oliver, but not from Agatha Christie. *Faust* was, in fact, not played at Covent Garden after the war until the 1970s. The girls must have been taken to Sadler's Wells. Opera is mentioned earlier in the same novel, when a letter is written saying: 'Dear Baron von Eisenger. We can certainly arrange for Hedwig to go to the Opera on the occasion of Hellstern's taking the roll [sic] of Isolda —'

This opera is mentioned again in *The Sittaford Mystery* (*Murder at Hazlemoor*), but only in passing: 'He looked, Emily thought, as Tristan ought to look in the third act of *Tristan and Isolde* and as no Wagnerian tenor has ever looked yet.'

Such references to music are characteristic: casual, nonchalant, not embedded in the story. On other occasions, the author uses musical terms in a similar fashion. In *Dead Man's Folly*, the butler rings the gong in 'a most artistic performance, *crescendo, forte, diminuendo, rallentando* . . .' In *The Moving Finger*, the barely convalescent narrator is warned, musically if inaccurately, by his doctor: 'You've got to take life slowly and easily, the *tempo* is marked *Legato*.'

But in a few novels, music plays a more important role. The murder weapon in *They Do It With Mirrors* is concealed in the piano stool, where less frequently played pieces are kept. First Inspector Curry examines the music out on the instrument itself, and is expectedly amazed: 'Hindemith? Who's he? Never heard of him. Shostakovitch! What names these people have!' Then he looks into the stool.

'Here's the old-fashioned stuff. Handel's *Largo*, Czerny's *Exercises*, "I know a lovely garden" – Vicar's wife used to sing that when I was a boy —'

The automatic is lying on Chopin's *Preludes*. One wonders, parenthetically, how the pianist managed to play Hindemith and Shostakovitch if he neglected his Czerny so badly.

In *Hercule Poirot's Christmas* music plays a significant role; two alibis are based on it. David, the vague and unsatisfactory son of the family, who 'always got on father's nerves . . . with his music', plays the piano after dinner. The 'Dead March' (does the author mean the march from Handel's *Saul* or the third movement of the Chopin Second Piano Sonata?). The point of his playing is that it seems to cover the time during which his father is murdered (and nobody else in the house could play either Handel or Chopin). During that same time, two lovers of less austere music, in another part of the house, are dancing to a gramophone. Since the gramophone, too, is heard constantly, they obviously do not have time – in that pre-LP age – to rush upstairs and do the deed.

In one of her novels, Agatha Christie speaks of 'variations on a well-known theme'. This might be a description of the body of her own work. Whether her characters – victims, suspects or villains – like music or not is immaterial; she obviously enjoyed its formality as something kin to her own. And even in her constant use of nursery rhymes and old songs there is a hint at her work's general quality, for it has – in the original sense – a 'popular' tone. No doubt, most of her characters are rich or well-to-do (and the poor ones always have at least one maid), but still these novels are the finest 'people's' literature in a way that works of Soviet or People's Republic orthodox hacks can never achieve.

As a postscript to these observations on music in Agatha Christie, which make no claim to completeness by the way, one must mention a novel she wrote in her other, more romantic, less formal persona, Mary Westmacott. This is *Giant's Bread*, and – poles away from the Christie canon – the entire story revolves around artists, the most important being a singer (who loses her voice) and a composer (who loses the singer).

This is a remarkable book. Written in 1930, it comes some time after other 'composer' novels like Henry Handel Richardson's *Maurice Guest* and Romain Rolland's mammoth *Jean-Christophe*, which may well have influenced it. Music, in *Giant's Bread*, is not a form of entertainment, not a source of pleasure, not even an artistic discipline: it is a kind of possession, or rather obsession, which seizes its foreordained victim and forces him to follow it.

Vernon, the composer of the story, 'gets music' the way some people get religion. Dragged against his will to a concert (the time is some years before World War I), he is bowled over. Admittedly, it is a special sort of concert, as he describes it: 'There were nine orchestras . . . all massed. Sound can be glorious if you get enough of it. I don't mean just loudness – it shows more when it's soft. But there must be enough. I don't know what they played – nothing, I think, that was real . . .'

From this experience he envisages a music of the future: 'I want to know every instrument there is. What it can do, what are its limitations, what are its possibilities. And the notes, too. There are notes they don't use – notes they ought to use.'

Incoherent at first, Vernon's ideas about music grow clearer. In a striking passage, the author says: 'He drew an experimental finger round the edge of his finger bowl. Jo shuddered and clapped both hands to her ears. The sound increased in volume. Vernon smiled dreamily and ecstatically.

'"One ought to be able to catch that and harness it. I wonder how it could be done. It's a lovely round sound, is it? Like a circle."'

The answer to Vernon's rhetorical question is: tape. Sounds of glasses ('Let's have the Venetian and the Waterford together,' he says a bit farther on) and of tins and automobiles were – several decades later – to be harnessed on tape, manipulated, and turned into *musique concrète*.

Vernon thinks of four-dimensional music; but in fact, he begins at once by writing an opera. His mind works in dramatic terms: 'Suddenly he saw the whole thing in music – the high tower and the princess's cascade of golden hair, and the eerie haunting tune of the prince's pipe which called the princess out of the tower . . . He heard the music of the tower – the round globular music of the princess's jewels . . .'

The tower makes one think again of *Pelléas*, though there is also a hint of Delius. And the question springs naturally to mind: is Vernon based on a real composer? A musical friend and fellow-Agathian has suggested Arthur Bliss, not only because his dates are right (1891-1975) but also because he wrote the music for H. G. Wells's films of the future. Prokofiev – of the *Pas d'acier* – is also a possibility. Personally, I was reminded at times of Scriabin, of that artist's compulsion to go beyond the restrictions and confines of traditional music expression. Today one might think of still more advanced inventors: Xenakis, Cage. The fact is that, on the basis of her voice studies and her piano lessons, Mary Westmacott created an extraordinary, anti-conventional, but not unrealistic composer. And the study of the singer, who deliberately forces her small voice into a dangerous repertory (Wagner, Strauss's *Elektra*, and Vernon's own first opera) is equally compelling.

Several operas are discussed in the book, besides Vernon's. And one. the imaginary Radmaager's *Peer Gynt*, affords an unusual Westmacott–Christie cross-reference, because in *The Mystery of the Blue Train* a new opera is mentioned: *Peer Gynt*. But this time the composer's name is Claud Ambrose.

Giant's Bread opens with a prologue, which is actually a postlude to the novel's action. The brief chapter describes the opening night of 'London's new National Opera House' with *The Giant*. It is an extremely daring work, and one section of the orchestra is called 'The Glass' ('in the new modern phrase'). It deeply impresses Carl Bowerman, 'the most distinguished of English musical critics' (is he

Ernest Newman?). But the audience reaction is mixed. As the author says of it: '"Why can't they open a British opera house with a decent British composer? [Vernon has assumed a foreign pseudonym.] All this Russian tomfoolery!" Thus a peppery colonel.'

One wonders: is the peppery colonel our old friend Major Blunt, now promoted? And further: is Miss Marple perhaps in the audience? If so, she probably dislikes the opera, which reminds her, no doubt, of something that happened to the vicar . . .

Christianna Brand
Miss Marple - A Portrait

AGATHA CHRISTIE once described to me her own particular method of getting down to work. She mulled over a book in her mind till it was ready, she said – well, we all do that – and she would then repair to a *very bad hotel*. In a bad hotel, there was nothing to do but to write, and plenty of time to do it in. The beds were so uncomfortable that you had no inclination to retire early or to get up late, the armchairs so unyielding that you wasted not a minute in idle relaxation. The meals were so bad that there was no temptation to linger over them, and any guests who would put up with such conditions must of necessity be so stupid that you couldn't possibly make friends and spend precious moments in desultory chat. So the book would be done in a matter of weeks and you could pack up the few dull clothes which were all you need bother to take with you, and go off triumphantly home.

I never heard of anyone else to whom she confided this ploy, nor have I ever heard that in fact it was the way she worked. So either she was making it up or I am. For myself, I do most positively swear that I distinctly recall the conversation; however, *nil nisi bonum* – I daresay it's me that's wrong.

True or false, there was one fellow guest upon whom – whatever the surroundings – Mrs Christie would certainly have fallen with cries of joy. Miss Marple inclined to the comforts of Brown's – I mean Bertram's – Hotel, or to the exotic pleasures of tropical islands, all laid on by kind nephew, Raymond West. But there may have been occasions when even Raymond's judgement faltered and he landed his dear Aunt Jane in some less propitious holiday setting, such as the bad hotel. She will certainly never have disillusioned him. He was, after all, so very generous and good and Miss Marple was adept at pulling the wool over eyes less sharply suspicious than her own.

Mrs Christie may well for a moment have mistaken the guest for her own grandmother, whom Miss Marple strongly resembled: a tall, thin old lady with soft white curling hair, a pink and white face and an expression of the utmost gentleness in her china blue eyes – somewhat unfairly belying, I have often thought, the extreme cynicism of her outlook on human nature. This had been formed presumably in the pre-natal condition, for she sprang fully armed with it into life, at the age of seventy-four; continuing almost as closely enwombed for the rest of her days in the small village of St Mary Mead – a sink of petty iniquity if ever there was one – until at an age which we cannot but ungallantly assess as well over the hundred mark, her career came to a close. With the death of her creator – even at eighty-five untimely – Hercule Poirot has also died. But in the final book tucked up her posthumous sleeve, Mrs Christie has left Miss Marple to simply fade softly away. Perhaps she could not bear to kill off her own grandmother.

Miss Marple will have been knitting when Mrs Christie came upon her in the bad hotel. The uncomfortable chairs, I dare say, won't have been troubling her; she would sit very upright, 'having been trained on a backboard in her youth and taught not to loll' – and never for a moment would her hands have been idle. 'Something fleecy' would have been forming on her knitting needles – what in the world she can have done with all she produced, one simply can't imagine: she had a tendency, certainly, to embark upon small matinée coats before even the prospective parents themselves suspected the approach of the Little Stranger, but her acquaintances naturally tended to be beyond child-bearing age. (One does hope, rather anxiously, that all that excessive fleeciness wasn't something of a threat to infant lungs; what with Miss Marple's own hair which was known to be fleecy in itself and all those fleecy shawls she wore, never mind the fleeciness of the inevitable knitting, the very air about her must have been full of flying particles of nasally irritating fluff.)

At any rate, she knitted. No sunshine was too radiantly brilliant, no sea too sparkling blue, no lamplight too softly beaming – for Miss Marple to whip out her knitting bag and start off, clickety-click. Even an evening party seems not to have been sacred and if the knitting came to an end, there was always the crochet hook handy and off she went again. Her outlay in wool must have eaten up every penny saved up by her ladylike economies. Thank goodness nephew Raymond, that well-to-do literary young man, not to say precious young prig, was always there to pay for the sunshine holidays! No doubt many a fleecy pullover rewarded him – never to be surreptitiously disposed of, 'consciously debonair' though we know him to have been; for Aunt Jane would obviously have expected to see her offerings sported upon the manly chest and would by no means have been deceived by fibs about dishonest servants or the depredations of the rapacious moth. 'Now that reminds me so much of dear Jane Helier,' she would have said, with those bursts of italics, which in her conversation made up for a considerable lack of other punctuation,

'. . . the film star you know, dear boy, such a pretty young woman but not very *clever*, these theatrical people so often are *not* and I understand that in the film world, they are hardly required to be, some person called the director or producer, I'm not sure which, does it all for them . . . But where was I? (Just a moment, dear, while I count this row, I fear I may have dropped a stitch . . .) Yes, I was saying that poor dear Jane was given such a dreadful garment, a woollen *jumper* I think it would be called nowadays though I never quite understand *why*, and some admirer, some fan, as Jane would say, had knitted it for her but of course in her position it was impossible to wear such a thing and she gave it away to a jumble sale, but the Vicar's wife, perhaps not very *honestly*, dear, considering her situation, but then again they are so very badly paid even nowadays, Vicars, I mean, not their wives who of course are not paid at all which does seem wrong when you think of all that is expected of them . . . Well, as I was saying, on this occasion she thought it a fair enough exchange, I dare say, to give her her due, if she kept the garment for herself and put in a worn jumper of her *own*. And then of course the next time the poor donor went to Evensong, well, there was the Vicar's wife in the very garment she had so laboriously knitted for her idol. As I say, poor dear Jane is *not* very clever, or she wouldn't have given the thing to a *local* charity . . .

And she would have fixed dear Raymond with that deceptively gentle blue eye. 'But then, of course, I fear that you are *not* a church-goer, my dear boy?' she would have said with the just acceptable admixture of reproach and regret – not to mention suspicion – as she glanced at the smooth, decidedly machine-made article just visible beneath his hastily buttoned-up jacket. 'You would have been exposed to no such unfortunate impulses.'

Did Mrs Christie as the years went by, fall a little out of love with M. Poirot? Is it possible, as some have claimed, that in fact she never loved him at all? She created Miss Marple, at any rate, as his very antithesis. Where Poirot is all shine and show-off, Miss Marple is the very pink of modest self-deprecation: how totally sincerely we may sometimes wonder for she certainly has a quiet confidence in her own powers, robustly bolstered up, should it ever fail her, by the adulation of her somewhat unremarkable friends. She and M. Poirot share, it is true, a tendency, sometimes bordering on the criminal, to play their cards very close indeed to their chests, repressing the solution to some progressively monstrous sequence of crimes, till the moment arrives when they may sun themselves in triumphant unravellings.

In this, however, they are hardly alone among the literary detective fraternity. It has been done, but it cannot be often that a reader had been kept enthralled throughout a couple of hundred pages, by the slow unmasking of a multiple murderer whose identity, motive and method have been outlined in Chapter One. Of Miss Marple it must in honour be said that she is a great deal more scrupulous in this matter than the gentleman of the little grey cells. The reader may be kept in the dark, but accredited investigators are forewarned in a note scribbled on a scrap of paper and quietly pressed into the official palm: the name written therein, having been withheld from the rest of the characters, only out of a laudable anxiety that damaging accusations be not broadcast until their truth has been absolutely proven. Such broad hints as, 'I am reminded so much of Mrs Smith's little housemaid at home in St Mary Mead, who never *could* distinguish between *mushrooms* and *toadstools*,' may be trusted to pass completely over their heads. It must be confessed that most of Miss Marple's friends are less than liberally equipped with any share of the little grey cells.

Nor has the lady herself great pretensions in that quarter, as she would be the first to acknowledge. A strong appetite for village gossip of a paralysingly boring nature, an aptitude for total recall of the information so gleaned and an almost paranoid mistrust of her fellow men and especially of her fellow women – these are her stock in trade. And it is by comparison with very small events, that she tumbles to immense conclusions: put a droplet of water under a microscope, so runs her message, and you will find there a teeming life, even though the water comes only from a village pond. Nor is the source to be despised. 'Talking scandal,' she admits, going a little pink, '– well, it's done a good deal. And people are very down on it – especially clever young people . . .' (The clever young person in the back of Miss Marple's mind is in fact kind, but highly critical not to say often censorious, nephew Raymond West.) 'But what I say is that none of these young people ever stop to *think*. They really don't examine the facts. Surely the whole crux of the matter is this: *How often is tittle tattle*, as you call it, *true*! And I think if, as I say, they really examined the facts they would find it was true nine times out of ten! That's really just what makes people so annoyed about it!'

'The inspired guess,' suggests one of her listeners.

'No, not that, not that at all! It's really a matter of practice and

Margaret Rutherford, the best known of all Miss Marples, through such films as *Murder She Said* (*above*) and *Murder Ahoy* (*right*). Despite her dissimilarity to the author's conception of Miss Marple, it is Miss Rutherford's characterization that has prevailed over all others.

experience. . . . What I'm trying to say – very badly, I know – is this:
What my nephew – ' (I told you!) ' – calls "superfluous women" have
a lot of time on their hands, and their chief interest is *people*. And so,
you see, they get to be what one might call *experts*. Now, young people
nowadays – they talk very freely about things that weren't mentioned
in my young days, but on the other hand their minds are terribly
innocent. They believe in everyone and everything. And if one tries
to warn them, ever so gently, they tell one that one has a Victorian
mind – and that, they say, is like a *sink*.'

Yet after all, suggests another listener – falling all too understand-
ably into Miss Marple's habit of emphasis – what is wrong with a
sink?

'Exactly. It's the most necessary thing in any house. . . .'

Not content with the scum from other people's sinks, Miss Marple
is vigilant to equip her own and to this end does not disdain to spend
a good deal of time at open windows – wrapped in a sufficiency of the
fleecy shawls, we may be sure – with a pair of binoculars glued to her
china blue eyes: all ready, should she be disturbed, to have had a
charm of goldfinches in her sights just a moment ago. To observe
the butcher's boy pedalling by with his load in a basket fixed to his
handle-bars, is to be reminded most aptly at some future date, of the
fact that nowadays they use only those horrid *wooden* skewers, so
difficult to get back once one has removed them from the joint; so
that if a poor old woman is found dead, transfixed through the heart
with a *steel* one, the recent movements of any old-fashioned purveyor
of meat should be enquired into urgently. On so frail a thread has
many a malefactor hanged by the neck in the earlier days of Miss
Marple's activities; and who shall say that the sequence of events is
not always logical and – allowing for a somewhat large margin of
alternative interpretation – quite likely to be correct. True, most of
us cherish a skewer or two on the dear old original pattern for poking
down choked drains – back to the sink again! – and would be as likely
suspects if this were all, as the traditional butcher; but it is never
safe to underrate Agatha Christie. Subtly led to put all our faith in the
coincidence of the metal skewer and old-world charcuterie, we shall
find that, after all, the skewer was just one which the aged eccentric
was accustomed to use in a high wind to secure her hat, and had
merely come in handy in a case of unpremeditated murder; and that,
all the time, it was recollection of the butcher boy's *basket* that had

alerted Miss Marple to the fact that the old lady's was missing. If the old lady carried no basket then she could not have been going out shopping as everyone had assumed and must therefore have been lured out on some other pretext by her murderer – too much to hope that it was the *situation* of the boy's basket that had led to Miss Marple's flash of intuition regarding a villain with *handle-bar moustaches*. But one way or another – on to the eventual unmasking . . .

Everything, in other words, reminds Miss Marple of some small occurrence in St Mary Mead which may subsequently be matched against events in the world outside. It is usually accepted, however, that these deductions play a greater part in her detective work than in fact they do. The connection between the butcher boy's basket and arrival at the solution to the mystery is, after all, tenuous in the extreme, but it is a good enough comparison with Miss Marple's accustomed processes of thought – though not an actual example. Mrs Christie's sleight of hand is seldom less than miraculous, her deductive procedure impeccable; but of Miss Marple and her methods, Dr Johnson might well have observed that it was not so much that the thing was well done as that it had been done at all – (and by a lady aged anywhere between seventy-four and a hundred and one.)

In several of the longer novels, she deserts St Mary Mead almost entirely. No erring errand boy, no unseemly seamstress leaps unbidden to her mind. Instead she leans – a little more heavily than in matters of such huge importance, many of us would perhaps dare to do – upon the sort of sixth sense that reads truth or falsehood in people's eyes (though exceedingly well able to dissemble it in her own) – sees guilt in the set of their mouths, recognizes worlds of meaning in their manner or deportment. She goes even further. So important a person as 'a Confidential Adviser to the Home Office' places a quite extra-ordinary reliance upon the suggestion that she has 'a very fine sense of evil'. Miss Marple does not disclaim. It's true, she agrees, that on several occasions she has 'recognised that there was evil in the neighbourhood, the surroundings, that the environment of someone who was evil was near me, connected with what was happening'. She has 'a kind of emotional reaction or susceptibility to – well, I can only call it atmosphere . . . It's rather, you know, like being with a very keen sense of smell. You can smell a leak of gas when other people can't do so. You can distinguish one perfume from another very easily'. (With St Mary Mead, it will be observed, Miss Marple's italics are also left behind; and even something of her grammatical accuracy too.) 'I had an aunt once who said she could smell when people told a lie. She said there was quite a distinctive odour came to her. Their noses twitched, she said, and then the smell came.' Sherlock Holmes might have suggested that this phenomenon would be likely to occur in the reverse order, but then he was aridly free of the sort of atmospheric pressures which came increasingly to govern Miss Marple's otherwise rather matter-of-fact outlook – though at least as liberal in his deductions from the mud splash on the outside of the left boot or the missing button indicative of the missing wife, as ever Miss Marple would have dared to be. And it must be said at once that she by no means relied exclusively upon otherworldly powers of insight but, having let her sensitive nose point the way, stood aside and allowed her creator to back it all up with some good, thumping, red-blooded clues. Where Jane Marple went, Agatha Christie was never far behind. Together they make an absolutely unbeatable pair.

Well – Dame Agatha, alas, has gone. But she has left with us that pseudo-grandmother with all her manifold comic little charms – the gentle blue eyes that could cast so suspicious a glance, the soft pink cheeks flushing up with the horrid excitement of the chase; the fleecy white hair which occasionally turned back to grey, the failing eyesight which never deterred her from keenly observing, not to say occasion-ally downright spying, the increasing deafness which interfered not at all with the habit of eavesdropping, the twinges of rheumatism, the severer onset of arthritis, which still did not deter her from setting forth upon adventures which might have daunted many a centenarian less incapacitated than herself.

Dear Miss Marple! – with her fleecy pink and white knitting (re-placed by a scarf in purple crochet when any recent tragedy of a felonious nature suggested to her Victorian sense of propriety that a sort of half-mourning would be more fitting) – and her small, elegant economies. Miss Marple visited no picture galleries on her excursions to London (at nephew Raymond's expense) and went to no museums, and 'the idea of patronising a dress show of any kind would never have occurred to her' – any more than, perhaps, to a good many of us. But she was fond of a ramble round the china and linen departments of the great stores, keeping a sharp look-out for anything 'marked down'. It is agreeable to know that at our final parting, we leave her with no such cheese-paring necessities . . .

For in *Nemesis*, the last book actually to have been written about her – the last to be published had been written many years before – arrangements for her future comfort have been most handsomely laid on. A proposition is set before her, which seems to leave her with very little information; or indeed, it may well seem to the astonished reader, any information whatsoever. The proposer, in a posthumous letter, recalls her, perhaps not surprisingly, as likely to be spending her time mainly in knitting – harking back to a moment of danger when she appeared at his bedside 'in a cloud of pink wool' charmingly described as a fascinator. (It must be hastily added that Miss Marple's appearance at any gentleman's bedside, with or without a fascinator, would be the rarest of events; and would constitute in itself no threat whatsoever.) But it was then, the writer declares, that it became apparent to him – as in the same book it later becomes apparent to the Confidential Adviser to the Home Office aforementioned – that she has 'a natural *flair* for justice, which in turn has led to a natural *flair* for crime'. He is accordingly bequeathing to her a sum of money – which proves to be no less than twenty thousand pounds – if she will successfully investigate a certain crime. As to what the crime is or what persons may be involved, he gives no hint at all, nor any sug- gestion as to how she may go about finding out for herself; he is wryly determined, it seems, to confound any possible curiosity on the part of the acting solicitor, and to this end denies her any word that might be useful to her in the proposed undertaking. But Miss Marple, though she repudiates the legal gentleman's suggestions as to possible expenditure of the legacy once earned – a *cruise*, one of those excellent *tours* that can nowadays be arranged, replenishment of one's cellars – does confess to very much enjoying a partridge, a whole partridge to oneself! – and a box of *marrons glacés* is an expensive taste which she has not hitherto been able to indulge. Possibly one might even treat oneself to a visit to the opera, entailing as that does a car to Covent Garden and back, and the cost of a night at an hotel (no doubt, though she does not confide this thought also, one could spend the following day before the *first class* travel back to St Mary Mead, in the linen and china shops, revelling in the luxury of not having to watch out for reductions). So – the thought of the twenty thousand pounds is irresistible. Without one word as to how she is even to begin to go about it, Miss Marple accepts the challenge. And of course, inspiration comes, nebulous in the extreme indeed, but Miss Marple is off and into the upper air. 'It seemed to me that there was an atmosphere there of sorrow, of deep-felt unhappiness, also an atmosphere of fear and a kind of struggling different atmosphere which I can only describe as an atmosphere of normality.'

'Your last word interests me,' says the Adviser to the – well, you know who.

It was not entirely the last word. The last word has since appeared in a book written long before Miss Marple had come to this just reward. But she has it at least, and we leave her lapped in comfort. And what is so lovely is that she's going to spend it *all*. We know of no other member of the family to whom she feels any obligation to make bequests in her turn, and nephew Raymond is, as he always has been, well enough provided for – and moreover in middle age is becoming so increasingly pompous and pleased with himself, as it seems to me, and more than necessarily unkind about Aunt Jane's little foibles, that even she must be growing a little less fondly indulgent; I'm glad that from now on she'll be independent of his holiday treats. And she will. 'There is no point in saving at my age,' she assures the protesting solicitors – who but a moment ago were pressing upon her those luxurious cruises, let alone stocking up on wines and spirits, but are now apparently growing apprehensive as to an onset of riotous living. 'I mean, the point is to enjoy the things one never thought one would have the money to enjoy.' To murmurings as to a possible rainy day – at the age of a hundred and one? – she replies with a touch of her old asperity that all she will need for a rainy day, will be her umbrella. 'I'm going to spend this money. I'm going to have some fun with it.'

With all our hearts, having had so much fun with *her* – we will hope that she does.

H.R.F. Keating
Hercule Poirot - A Companion Portrait

HERCULE POIROT, the greatest sleuth (bar one) ever to stalk his prey through the body-littered pages, was born, I calculate, in 1844, only fourteen years after his native Belgium had broken away from Holland to become an independent kingdom. He died full of years, very full of years, in 1974, the circumstances of his demise – bizarre as even he, connoisseur of bizarre decease, could have wished – being reported some twelve months later as soon as his chronicler of old, Captain Arthur Hastings, could bring himself to set down the astonishing facts. Poirot departed this life then aged 130, or perhaps a bit more. It depends how old he is likely to have been when he retired, full of honour, from the Belgian Police in, we are told, 1904. A vigorous sixty then would have made him only 130, a more mature sixty-five would have brought him finally to 135, within sight indeed of all-time winner Abraham's 'a hundred three score and fifteen years'. But no one can tell. Poirot was always a little touchy on the subject of age. Precise figures are not to be found.

Not one of the records of his cases mentions dates definite enough to be of conclusive help. True, the affair of the *Dead Man's Mirror* begins with a letter from Sir Gervase Chevenix-Gore, of Hamborough Close, Hamborough St Mary (Station: Whimperley. Telegrams: Hamborough St John) dated 24 September 1936. And it is also possible to fix the date on which Poirot attended Sunday Matins while solving so brilliantly the case it is convenient to call *One, Two, Buckle My Shoe*, or in America *The Patriotic Murders*. This must have been on 29 January 1939 since he joined in singing, in a hesitant baritone (and no wonder as he was probably aged 104) in that week's Psalm 140. But mostly it is evidence such as the naming of a youth as Gary and the mention of a gardener's television set in *Dead Man's Folly* that enables us to say with conviction that his cases took place always about a year before the printed record was published.

So 1974 is the year of his final posthumous triumph, an affair that will be found to baffle with wonderful satisfaction almost everyone who reads it. It took place at Styles St Mary, scene of his first English murder. In my end is my beginning: it is fitting to quote T. S. Eliot, a poet who did not disdain to help himself verbatim from Conan Doyle's *The Musgrave Ritual* for his *Murder in the Cathedral*.

And Poirot's last words, whispered to his friend of many years, Captain Hastings, who had returned from the Argentine (at the youthful age, I estimate, of eighty-eight) were 'Cher ami'. They thus neatly echoed the very first recorded words of the great Belgian sleuth uttered in 1916 (ascertainable date), 'Mon ami, Hastings!' Hard upon them came the first description of the 'extraordinary looking little man'. We learn of his shortness of stature, 'hardly more than five feet four inches', of his way of nevertheless carrying himself with immense dignity, of the fact that his head was exactly the shape of an egg and that it was invariably perched a little to the left. And above all we learn of his moustaches, very stiff and military, waxed to the sharpest points, his pride and joy. And there was too the extreme neatness of his attire, indeed it is called 'almost incredible'. We hear no mention at this time of his green eyes, but later we come across them often enough, getting significantly greener when a clue (often delectably misleading) rose up and at times even shining like a cat's. But this was a phenomenon which in later, calmer days seems not to have been in evidence.

The extravagant gestures also escape mention at first encounter but later frequently horrify the staid English among whom the great detective came to spend his life. Occasionally (no, quite often) they are dextrously employed so as to knock over an ornament or similar object and thus prove something altogether startling. Once, a gesture more than usually ingenious, if a little hard to visualize, knocked off the pince-nez worn by the murderer's faithful female accomplice in such a manner that Poirot was able to replace them by a pair he knew to have been worn by the killer, thus confirming, when the good lady failed to notice the substitution, an already formed hypothesis.

Poirot's neatness was commented on at his first appearance, but it emerged only later that he almost invariably wore a correct black jacket, striped trousers and a bow-tie with, if the weather was anything less than hot, an overcoat and a muffler. And he had shiny boots, of patent leather, simultaneously acknowledging the paramount need to achieve a spotless appearance and declining to attain it in the properly British way, by the application of much polish and, if as was preferable a servant was doing the polishing, some spit. But those boots. How often our hero sacrificed their shininess in pursuing the criminal or in searching for some proof. Even when, in *Evil Under The Sun*, he substituted for them a pair of white suède shoes, which he wore with a suit of white duck and a panama hat, he found it necessary to besmirch their immaculateness by venturing almost to the edge of the sea. And how he hated the sea. It must have been only

the necessity of crossing it that prevented him extending his triumphant career to the far side of the Atlantic.

Under panama or correct bowler lay, brushed with enormous
exactitude, the hair which remained till his dying day an unrepentant
black. It must even under the panama in that summer immediately
before the Second World War have needed frequent applications of
'a tonic, not a dye', but for the significance of that jetty coiffure at the
very end you must read *Curtain: Poirot's Last Case* for yourself. It
produces not the least of the genuine and effective *coups de théâtre*
that enlivened the long, long career.

His manner of speech was as extravagant often as his gestures.
It has been said of him that he broke into French for the easy phrases
and was able to master English for the complex thoughts. But that
is unfair, if only a little. Certainly he retained his inability to capture
certain easy English idioms till the very end when he give us such
simple delights as 'the side of the bed manner', fit to stand beside
the early 'money for the *confiture*, as you say'. And from time to time
he did not forget to claim that his difficulties with English were in
part assumed. They made people look on him as a foreigner, he would
slyly point out, and thus someone in whom the outrageous could
safely be confided since all Englishmen believe foreigners are naturally outrageous anyway.

Indeed, his foreignness was an asset all round. Its comicality gave
him a proper quantum of the endearing as well as allowing him to be
invariably successful without becoming odious. He could boast too,
a useful accomplishment for the detective when matters are to be
explained. And he could listen at keyholes and read other people's
letters, things which no decent Englishman has ever been known to
do. But when his fearful foreignness brought him to the verge of
being altogether too ridiculous his being a Belgian foreigner rescued
him. He came, one would recall, from that sturdy 'gallant little'
country. He was all right. Let Mrs Platt-Hunter-Platt, as chronicled
in 1937 by Mr Michael Innes in *Hamlet, Revenge*, give tongue:
'There is a very good man whose name I forget, a foreigner and very
conceited – but, they say, thoroughly reliable.' English has no word
of greater praise for a fellow than that 'reliable'.

So Poirot became established in England, sharing London rooms
at 14 Farraway Street with the faithful Hastings and with a landlady
in attendance. He was conscious in these circumstances of certain

similarities with a famous forbear, though Hastings sprouted no sudden medical qualification but had a job as secretary to an MP (name unspecified and political affiliation ignored) and the landlady emerged from total anonymity – no superbly named Hudson she – only by obligingly never laying breakfast or tea things with perfect symmetry and thus enabling Poirot to give vent to a characteristic trait.

It was indeed at Farraway Street that Poirot paid his most explicit homage to his great forerunner, in the startling affair of *The Big Four*. At the height of that extraordinary case – well, it included not only a mysterious Chinaman, but darts tipped with fatal curare, a bid for world domination and as well an instant anaesthetic with, for good measure, the capture of faithful old Hastings by threatening to make away with his wife in a lingering fashion ('My God, you fiend') – Poirot announced that this was a matter so serious that it called for the intervention of his brother. 'Your brother,' Hastings cried in astonishment, 'I never knew you had a brother.' 'You surprise me, Hastings. Do you not know that all celebrated detectives have brothers who would be even more celebrated than they are were it not for constitutional indolence?' Thus Achille Poirot was born, to die in the last thrilling pages when it is revealed that Hercule had temporarily sacrificed even his moustaches in order to create him, much as a Mrs Christie might sacrifice her accustomed tone of steady probability for one wild *jeu d'esprit*, or, as Poirot might say, the game of the spirit.

Hastings, who had been banished by a happy marriage to South America, returned for this escapade. But, dear arch-bumbler, he was soon sent packing again. The classic Holmes–Watson pattern has the great advantage of enabling a story-teller to have a detective who sees all but credibly does not tell all, but it is inclined to limit the type of case open to him when everything has to be seen through a dull pair of eyes. All too soon a useful device can become fossilized into a music-hall act.

So Poirot established himself alone, except for a loyal manservant Georges to whom portentous phrases could be addressed at the height of a case without too much danger of any answering back. Poirot chose as his new domicile Whitehaven Mansions, a newly built block of flats pleasing to him for its extreme symmetry. At the beginning of *The Labours of Hercules* (somebody loved parallels, with classical stories, with nursery rhymes, with herself) after a little introductory matter explaining that Poirot now intended finally, finally, finally to retire but would like to end his career with twelve cases that happened to correspond to the twelve tasks that confronted his illustrious namesake, we read of his new abode (telephone: TRAfalgar 8137): 'Hercule Poirot's flat was essentially modern in its furnishings. It gleamed with chromium. Its easy-chairs, though comfortably padded, were square and uncompromising in outline.' And there was 'a piece of good modern sculpture representing one cube placed on another cube and above it a geometrical arrangement of copper wire'. How he worked at being the detective every decent Englishman loves to hate.

But, of course, he did not retire. As one can tell from that sculpture, money was now rolling in. There were dozens of juicy clients, mostly only hinted at – a Home Secretary or two, various millionaires, a few princes and 'the affair of the Ambassador's boots' (just a question of drug-smuggling, Poirot loftily explains). He could now indulge all his gastronomic whims to the full and would voluntarily round off a long dinner that had ended with Baba au Rhum not with your Englishman's glass of port but with, ugh, crème de cacao. And the *tisanes* and camomile tea which the fellow would insist on when he could not get the thick sweet chocolate which he preferred to 'your English poison': it was enough to make anybody throw down his seven and sixpence on the bookshop counter in sheer disgust.

With wealth came influence. Now, in the 1930s, at the peak of success, describing himself no longer as a private detective but as 'a consultant' and still always threatening final, final, final, final retirement, he had at the beck and the call, as he might have said, a small host of useful people. Of course, replacing Hastings as his chronicler with another dull dog narrator (though he was a medical man) in that affair which caused an unparalleled sensation in 1926, *The Murder of Roger Ackroyd*, was not exactly a success, except in literary terms. 'Some readers', said a certain Mrs Christie, 'have cried indignantly "Cheating", an accusation that I have had pleasure in refuting by calling attention to various turns of phrasing and careful wording.'

But for everyday assistance he now had the impeccably efficient Miss Lemon as secretary and if the rough work of detection was to be done the Home Office was always now ready to oblige with instant labour and the Chief Constable of almost every county was in his

debt. Major This or Colonel That was invariably ready to let this brilliant amateur in on an investigation, especially since they were generally conducting them themselves with more military panache than cerebral ingenuity. But most of Poirot's information came from Detective Inspector Japp of Scotland Yard, little dark, ferret-faced Jimmy Japp, as he is called when first we meet him at Styles Court. He too managed to go on tracking down criminals over an awesome length of time. More than thirty years after the first collaboration he was still at the Yard, though now a Chief Inspector (there's rapid promotion for you, and after all those successes for which Poirot had let him take the credit), though by that time he had learnt to say 'Monsieur' instead of 'Moosier'.

Versions of Poirot:
W. Smithson Broadhead's
portrait (*far left*) for
The Sketch, 1924;
Francis L. Sullivan's
'straight' interpretation
(*left*) in *Peril at End House*,
1940; Charles Laughton,
the most famous of Poirots
(*right*), 'entirely unlike
him, but a wonderful actor',
according to the detective's
creator; and Albert Finney,
the most recent version
(*below right*), in *Murder
on the Orient Express*,
1974, exactly fifty years
after Broadhead's portrait.

Perhaps it is right to add to the list of Poirot's affiliates Mrs
Ariadne Oliver, the celebrated author of detective stories, a lady who
bore a noticeable resemblance to that other celebrated crime author,
Dame Agatha Christie. And also had some distinct differences, such
as hair that was often windswept and a magnificent booming con-
tralto where Dame Agatha possessed, according to one of her bio-
graphers, 'a rather high soprano voice'. Poirot and Mrs Oliver
collaborated in a number of cases, *Dead Man's Folly*, *Third Girl*, and
Elephants Can Remember. This last, clearly describing a period not
long before its publication in 1972, recorded Poirot's penultimate
triumph. He would then have been about 127 and did complain from
time to time about the effects of age. But his 'little grey cells' – that
famous and eventually self-mocked phrase which became the term
for the brain adopted by a whole African tribe – were still in fine
working order and Poirot was still mightily proud of their powers.

Pride, even cockiness, was perhaps his chief characteristic. In
Murder in the Mews he himself says to the good Japp: 'If I committed
a murder you would not have the least chance of seeing how I set
about it,' a boast not to be fulfilled till the very curtain fell. But the
cockiness is not without justification. Poirot is truly shrewd. Listen
to him: 'To deceive deliberately – that is one thing. But to be so sure
of your facts, of your ideas and of their essential truth that details do
not matter – that, my friend, is a special characteristic of particularly
honest persons.' And there are dozens of other examples every bit
as perceptive.

The shrewdness sprang from an unalterable belief in the rational.
'We shall *know*! The power of the human brain, Hastings, is almost
unlimited.' And it is this constant appeal to the rational, expressed
or implied, that was perhaps the reason for the tremendous popularity
of the accounts of his adventures when the world outside was increasingly swept by gusts of irrationality.

'Order and method' was ever his cry. And, though on occasion he
might spot a clue which lesser investigators had missed, he vehem-
ently denounced frenzied searching for clues as such. As early as
Murder on the Links, his second recorded case, he asked the faithful
Hastings if he ever went fox-hunting. 'A bit.' 'But you did not descend
from your horse and run along the ground smelling with your nose
and uttering loud "Ow, ows"?' Hastings solemnly took the point,
though as a matter of recorded fact on at least two occasions later

Poirot did actually use his own nose in a plainly clue-hunting way, once indeed to smell the cigarette smoke that was not there, classic instance.

He liked to work by hitting on a series of 'little ideas'. That, he used to say, was the first stage. Then the second stage would come, when a little idea proved correct. 'Then I *know*!' It was usually at the 'little ideas' stage that he would produce one of those lists of marvellously obscure questions. Why did the paper bag which he had seized on from the drawing-room waste-paper basket smell of oranges? Simple. It had been brought into the room under pretext of containing oranges so that at the right moment it could be inflated and popped so as to sound like a pistol shot fired at a time when the murderer could not have got to the place where the murder happened.

Little ideas enabled Poirot to conquer one of the gravest problems that can face the Great Detective: how not to solve, since one is pretty well omniscient, each puzzle the moment its facts have been made clear. By having small, but always properly startling, successes early on Poirot could postpone the great success till decently near the end of the book. Then it was: 'Quick, Hastings. I have been blind, *imbécile*. Quick, a taxi.' On occasion he described himself as triple imbecile, and once he admitted to thirty-six times imbecile.

The rational in Poirot reflected a basic seriousness. 'I have a bourgeois attitude to murder. I disapprove of it.' He goes so far, in 'The Adventure of the Italian Nobleman', one of his shorter exploits, as to claim: 'Never do I pull the leg.' That was just not true: he used to tease poor gawping Hastings unmercifully.

Finally, as in the *Who's Who* which Poirot so frequently pulled from his shelves when a possibly illustrious client was observed approaching, let us list the great man's 'recreations'. They included bridge (one whole adventure, *Cards on the Table*, is ingeniously devoted to it and he has a characteristically shrewd observation about those women players who declare with total confidence 'And the rest are mine') and detective fiction, of which to judge by his remarks in *The Clocks* he was an omnivorous devourer.

But there is one other area of interest (to those of us of a later vintage than Poirot – and given that natal date who could be otherwise? – of almost mandatory importance, though it has yet to be included in the *Who's Who* questionnaire): 'sexual proclivities?' Well, Poirot was, of course, never married, but if we run along the ground smelling with the nose on that track various 'little ideas' do spring up. Why, for instance, was he quite so fond of a duffer like Captain Hastings? Hastings, naturally, bumbled through their long friendship in total innocence. 'The embrace', he remarked when in 'The Jewel Robbery at the Grand Metropolitan' Poirot had threatened to put his arms round him, 'was merely figurative – not a thing one is always sure of with Poirot.' Indeed, in *The Mysterious Affair at Styles* 'suddenly clasping me in his arms, he kissed me warmly on both cheeks'.

Next, snuffle up an attitude to the opposite sex which, set aside some conventional words of praise, was always apt to be indifferent (with the exception of that significantly ample figure the Countess Rossakoff, encountered in several of the adventures) and was more than once actively hostile. 'Histoire de femmes,' he exclaimed with biting contempt in the wake of the departing film star Mary Marvell in 'The Adventure of the Western Star'. Even more significantly in *After the Funeral* he observed with savage brevity: 'Women are never kind, though they can sometimes be tender.'

One type of woman, it comes now as no surprise to find, he was always ready to find tender. In the closing pages of *Murder on the Links* he solemnly advises Jack: 'Go to your mother.' Tell her everything, he urges. 'Your love for each other has been tested in the fire and not found wanting.' To the Dowager Duchess of Merton he declares: 'I comprehend the mother's heart.' To Lady Yardly, almost as well-born, he says with a low bow, and in simple French, 'Vous êtes bonne mère.' No wonder that when a few minutes later Lady Yardly was found senseless on the floor after her great diamond had vanished she was, in Hastings' words, 'aptly ministered to by Poirot, who is as good as a woman in these matters'.

But there is one more clue. Think about that passage in *Peril at End House* where, addressing the Modern Miss heroine, he says: 'To me the natural thing seems to have a coiffure high and rigid – so – and the hat attached with many hairpins – là-là-là-et là' executing four vicious jabs in the air. 'When the wind blew,' he added 'it was agony – it gave you the migraine.' Now has the 'little idea' progressed to the point of 'I know'? We shall never learn the answer. Poirot has taken his secret to the grave. And, of course, to know is the last thing we really want. Let him rest in peace, aged 130.

The Agatha Christie Titles

1920 *The Mysterious Affair at Styles* (Poirot)
1922 *The Secret Adversary*
1923 *Murder on the Links* (Poirot)
1924 *The Man in the Brown Suit*
1924 *Poirot Investigates* (short stories)
1925 *The Secret of Chimneys*
1926 *The Murder of Roger Ackroyd* (Poirot)
1927 *The Big Four* (Poirot)
1928 *The Mystery of the Blue Train* (Poirot)
1929 *The Seven Dials Mystery*
1929 *Partners in Crime* (short stories)

1930 *Murder at the Vicarage* (Miss Marple)
1930 *The Mysterious Mr Quin* (short stories)
1931 *The Sittaford Mystery* (US: *Murder at Hazlemoor*)
1932 *Peril at End House* (Poirot)
1932 *The Thirteen Problems* (Miss Marple short stories)
    (US: *The Tuesday Club Murders*)
1933 *Lord Edgware Dies* (Poirot) (US: *Thirteen at Dinner*)
1933 *The Hound of Death* (short stories)
1934 *Why Didn't They Ask Evans?* (US: *The Boomerang Clue*)
1934 *Murder on the Orient Express* (Poirot) (US: *Murder in the Calais Coach*)
1934 *The Listerdale Mystery* (short stories)
1934 *Parker Pyne Investigates* (short stories) (US: *Mr Parker Pyne – Detective*)
1935 *Three Act Tragedy* (Poirot) (US: *Murder in Three Acts*)
1935 *Death in the Clouds* (Poirot) (US: *Death in the Air*)
1935 *The A.B.C. Murders* (Poirot)
1936 *Murder in Mesopotamia* (Poirot)
1936 *Cards on the Table* (Poirot)

1937 *Dumb Witness* (Poirot) (US: *Poirot Loses A Client*)

1937 *Death on the Nile* (Poirot)

1937 *Murder in the Mews* (Poirot stories) (US: *Dead Man's Mirror*)

1938 *Appointment with Death* (Poirot)

1938 *Hercule Poirot's Christmas* (US: *Murder for Christmas*)

1939 *Murder Is Easy* (US: *Easy to Kill*)

1939 *Ten Little Niggers* (US: *And Then There Were None*)

1939 *The Regatta Mystery and Other Stories* (some Poirot, one Miss Marple)

1940 *Sad Cypress* (Poirot)

1940 *One, Two, Buckle My Shoe* (Poirot) (US: *The Patriotic Murders*)

1941 *Evil Under the Sun* (Poirot)

1941 *N or M?*

1942 *The Body in the Library* (Miss Marple)

1942 *The Moving Finger* (Miss Marple)

1943 *Five Little Pigs* (Poirot) (US: *Murder in Retrospect*)

1944 *Towards Zero*

1945 *Death Comes as the End*

1945 *Sparkling Cyanide* (US: *Remembered Death*)

1946 *The Hollow* (Poirot)

1947 *The Labours of Hercules* (Poirot short stories)

1948 *Taken at the Flood* (Poirot) (US: *There Is A Tide*)

1948 *Witness for the Prosecution and Other Stories* (one Poirot)

1949 *Crooked House*

1950 *Three Blind Mice and Other Stories* (four Miss Marples, three Poirots)

1950 *A Murder Is Announced* (Miss Marple)

1951 *They Came to Baghdad*

1951 *The Underdog and Other Stories* (Poirot)

1952 *Mrs McGinty's Dead* (Poirot)

1952 *They Do It With Mirrors* (Miss Marple) (US: *Murder With Mirrors*)

1953 *A Pocketful of Rye* (Miss Marple)

1953 *After the Funeral* (Poirot) (US: *Funerals Are Fatal*)

1954 *Destination Unknown* (US: *So Many Steps to Death*)

1955 *Hickory, Dickory, Dock* (Poirot) (US: *Hickory, Dickory, Death*)

1956 *Dead Man's Folly* (Poirot)

1957 *4.50 From Paddington* (Miss Marple) (US: *What Mrs McGillicuddy Saw!*)

1958 *Ordeal by Innocence*

1959 *Cat Among the Pigeons* (Poirot)

1960 *The Adventure of the Christmas Pudding and Other Stories*
      (six Miss Marples, five Poirots)
1961 *Double Sin and Other Stories* (four Poirots, two Miss Marples)
1961 *The Pale Horse*
1962 *The Mirror Crack'd from Side to Side* (Miss Marple)
1963 *The Clocks* (Poirot)
1964 *A Caribbean Mystery* (Miss Marple)
1965 *At Bertram's Hotel* (Miss Marple)
1966 *Third Girl* (Poirot)
1967 *Endless Night*
1968 *By the Pricking of My Thumbs*
1969 *Hallowe'en Party* (Poirot)

1970 *Passenger to Frankfurt*
1971 *The Golden Ball and Other Stories*
1971 *Nemesis* (Miss Marple)
1972 *Elephants Can Remember* (Poirot)
1974 *Postern of Fate*
1974 *Poirot's Early Cases*
1975 *Curtain : Poirot's Last Case*
1976 *Sleeping Murder* (Miss Marple)

The Contributors

Elizabeth Walter has been an editor at Collins Publishers since 1961 and has edited their Crime Club list since 1971. A distinguished writer of stories of the supernatural, she has had five volumes published of which *Come And Get Me* and *Dead Woman* are the latest.

Julian Symons was recently elected President of the Detection Club in succession to Agatha Christie. He is the author of a history of crime writing, *Bloody Murder*, of criminological studies and biographies and of numerous crime novels, among them *The Colour of Murder*, winner of the Crime Writers' Association prize for 1953. From 1958 to 1968 he was crime reviewer for the London *Sunday Times*.

Edmund Crispin has reviewed mystery novels in the London *Sunday Times* since 1968. Between 1944 and 1953 he wrote the eight detective stories which have given him a secure place in the annals of the genre.

Michael Gilbert has been a prolific author of crime novels and short stories since 1947 and is a partner in a Lincoln's Inn firm of solicitors. He is editor of the series Classics of Adventure and Detection published by Hodder & Stoughton.

Emma Lathen is the author of many highly praised mystery novels notable for their solid backgrounds of aspects of American business life, of which *Murder against the Grain* won the Crime Writers' Association Golden Dagger for 1967. Under the name R. B. Dominic there is also a series centred on the political life of Washington, equally noted for thorough research.

Colin Watson is the author of *Snobbery With Violence*, a study of the sociological aspects of the crime story from the 1920s to James Bond. As a crime novelist himself, he has produced a series of humorous mysteries centred on the fictional East Anglian town of Flaxborough.

Celia Fremlin is the author of twelve novels of suspense, of which *The Hours before Dawn* won an Edgar Allan Poe award from the Mystery Writers of America in 1959. A wartime interviewer for Mass Observation, the opinion sampling organization, she collaborated with the late Tom Hopkinson, its founder, in the recently published *Living through the Blitz*.

Dorothy B. Hughes has been a mystery critic for a quarter of a century chiefly for the *Los Angeles Times* and the *New York Herald Tribune*. Author of a dozen suspense novels, she is currently writing a biography of Erle Stanley Gardner.

J. C. Trewin is a Cornishman and theatre historian, who has been a London drama critic since 1934, with the *Illustrated London News* since 1946. He has written more than forty books and lectured extensively in Britain and abroad. A former literary editor of the *Observer*, he is a Fellow of the Royal Society of Literature and a Past-President of the Critics' Circle.

Philip Jenkinson is a film critic, researcher and consultant (most recently for *Hindenberg* and *Valentino*). He is a governor of the British Film Institute and co-author of the book *Celluloid Rock*. He was for long a presenter on BBC-TV's *Late Night Line-Up* and *Film Night*.

William Weaver reviews crime novels for the London *Financial Times* and also writes about music and theatre in Italy, where he has lived since 1947. He also writes regularly for the *International Herald Tribune* (Paris) and other Italian, British and American publications. His translations from the Italian have won the National Book Award in the USA and the John Florio Prize in Britain.

Christianna Brand wrote a number of distinguished detective stories in the years between 1941 and 1955 and has since been a regular, and prize-winning, author of crime short stories. The American critic, Anthony Boucher, said of her that to find her rivals in the subtleties of the trade one must turn to 'the greatest of the Great Names, Agatha Christie, John Dickson Carr . . .'

H. R. F. Keating has been crime books critic of the London *Times* since 1967. He is the author of *Murder Must Appetize*, a study of the detective stories of the 1930s, and of a series of crime novels featuring Inspector Ghote of the Bombay CID.

Index